CW00929395

STOICISM 101

FROM MARCUS AURELIUS AND EPICTETUS TO THE ROLE OF REASON AND *AMOR FATI*, AN ESSENTIAL PRIMER ON STOIC PHILOSOPHY

ERICK CLOWARD, Host of the *Stoic Coffee Break* Podcast

ADAMS MEDIA

NEW YORK   AMSTERDAM/ANTWERP   LONDON   TORONTO   SYDNEY   NEW DELHI

Adams Media
An Imprint of Simon & Schuster, LLC
100 Technology Center Drive
Stoughton, Massachusetts 02072

First Adams Media hardcover edition February 2025

ADAMS MEDIA and colophon are registered trademarks of Simon & Schuster, LLC.

For information about special discounts for bulk purchases, please contact Simon &
Schuster Special Sales at 1-866-506-1949 or business@simonandschuster.com.

The Simon & Schuster Speakers Bureau can bring authors to your live event. For more
information or to book an event, contact the Simon & Schuster Speakers Bureau at
1-866-248-3049 or visit our website at www.simonspeakers.com.

Manufactured in the United States of America

1 2024

Library of Congress Cataloging-in-Publication Data
Names: Cloward, Erick, author.
Title: Stoicism 101 / Erick Cloward, host of the Stoic Coffee Break Podcast.
Other titles: Stoicism one hundred and one
Description: First Adams Media hardcover edition. | Stoughton, Massachusetts: Adams
Media, 2025. | Series: Adams 101 series | Includes index.
Identifiers: LCCN 2024040265 | ISBN 9781507223574 (hc) | ISBN 9781507223581
(ebook)
Subjects: LCSH: Stoics.
Classification: LCC B528 .C56 2025 | DDC 188--dc23/eng/20240924
LC record available at https://lccn.loc.gov/2024040265

ISBN 978-1-5072-2357-4
ISBN 978-1-5072-2358-1 (ebook)

CONTENTS

INTRODUCTION   7

THE STOIC MOVEMENT 9

ZENO OF CITIUM 14

SENECA THE YOUNGER 18

SENECA ON TIME MANAGEMENT 22

EPICTETUS 26

MARCUS AURELIUS 30

MARCUS AURELIUS'S *MEDITATIONS* 35

THE DICHOTOMY OF CONTROL 40

APPLYING THE DICHOTOMY OF CONTROL
IN EVERYDAY LIFE 44

VIRTUE 48

WISDOM 52

COURAGE 56

JUSTICE 60

TEMPERANCE 64

CHARACTER 68

IMPRESSIONS AND ASSENT 72

THE ROLE OF PERSPECTIVE IN STOICISM 77

THE STOIC "VIEW FROM ABOVE" 81

FREEDOM FROM EXTERNAL EVENTS 86

EUDAIMONIA 90

STOICISM ON WEALTH, FAME,
AND EXTERNAL GOODS 94

ACHIEVING *EUDAIMONIA* 98

THE *LOGOS* 102

LIVING ACCORDING TO NATURE. 106

APATHEIA. 110

EMOTIONAL RESILIENCE AND ACCEPTANCE 114

TECHNIQUES FOR MANAGING EMOTIONS 119

THE STOIC RESPONSE TO ANGER, ANXIETY,
  AND SADNESS 123

OIKEIÔSIS 127

COMPASSION AND EMPATHY IN STOICISM 131

THE ROLE OF RATIONALITY IN EMOTIONAL LIFE 135

THE ROLE OF SUFFERING 139

AMOR FATI 143

STOICISM'S INFLUENCE ON CHRISTIAN ETHICS 147

STOICISM AND MODERN PSYCHOLOGY. 152

THE CRITIQUE OF STOICISM 156

MEMENTO MORI 160

PRESENCE AND MINDFULNESS 164

STOICISM IN PERSONAL DEVELOPMENT
  AND SELF-HELP 168

STOICISM IN THE WORKPLACE AND LEADERSHIP . . .172

OUR HUMAN CONTRACT 176

STOICISM AND RELATIONSHIPS 180

THE UNIVERSE IS CHANGE 185

CARE FOR THE BODY 190

STOICISM AND THE ROLE OF PHYSICAL EXERCISE
  AND DISCIPLINE 195

SELF-ACCEPTANCE. 200

COMPARISON WITH OTHERS 204

HOW TO DEAL WITH ENEMIES 209

REPUTATION. 213

DEALING WITH CRITICISM 217

NO OPINION 221

RESILIENCE 226

STOICISM AND GOALS. 230

MORAL CONSISTENCY. 235

PREMEDITATIO MALORUM 240

GRATITUDE 245

CONSISTENCY 250

MORNING AND EVENING REFLECTIONS 254

STOIC THOUGHTS ON LOVE. 259

STOIC OPTIMISM. 263

INDEX   267

INTRODUCTION

In the bustling heart of the ancient Greek world, a profound philosophy took root that would endure through the ages, influencing millions with its wisdom and practicality. This philosophy is Stoicism, founded in the early third century B.C.E. by Zeno of Citium. At its core, Stoicism teaches the pursuit of virtue and wisdom as the path to true happiness, advocating for a life lived in harmony with reason and nature.

Stoicism is more than just a set of philosophical ideas; it is a way of life. Unlike many other philosophies, Stoicism is not about answering the grand philosophical questions of life; rather, it focuses on how to live a good life. It offers guidance on how to navigate the complexities and challenges of existence with grace and resilience, and cultivate inner tranquility and strength, regardless of fate or fortune.

Throughout this book, you'll learn about the Stoics' perspective and ideas about how to face the practical challenges of life such as:

- Why is it important to understand what is within your control and what is not?
- How do you maintain control of your emotions while dealing with the challenges of life?
- Why is it important to acknowledge the reality of your mortality?
- How should you treat other people?

- How can you develop resilience in the face of adversity and turn obstacles into opportunities for growth?
- And more.

Stoicism 101 aims to explore the rich tapestry of Stoic philosophy, from its ancient origins to its modern reappearance. Through the teachings of its most prominent figures, such as Seneca, Epictetus, and Marcus Aurelius, you'll learn how Stoicism outlines a path to achieving personal freedom and happiness by living according to virtue and rationality. As you delve into the principles and practices of Stoicism, you will discover how its timeless wisdom can be applied to your life today, offering insights into how to lead a more purposeful and serene life.

Whether you are encountering Stoicism for the first time or seeking to deepen your understanding, learning more about this ancient and enduring philosophy promises to be both enlightening and transformative, inviting you to view the world differently. Now turn the page to begin.

THE STOIC MOVEMENT

Origins and Development

Stoicism, one of the most influential schools of Greek and Roman philosophy, has profoundly shaped Western thought and continues to offer practical wisdom for modern life. Stoicism began in Athens, Greece, and later expanded to Rome and the Roman Empire.

ORIGINS OF STOICISM

Stoicism began in Athens, Greece, a fertile ground for philosophical thought. It had many influences, ultimately evolving into its current form. Read on to examine some of the major philosophical influences.

Zeno of Citium

Stoicism was founded by Zeno of Citium around 300 B.C.E. in Athens. Zeno, originally a wealthy merchant, turned to philosophy after losing his fortune in a shipwreck. Seeking guidance, he studied under various philosophers, which significantly influenced his thinking and the development of Stoic principles.

Socratic Influence

Socrates, a classical Greek philosopher, profoundly influenced Zeno and the philosophical school of Stoicism. Socrates emphasized the importance of virtue and knowledge, advocating for a life guided by reason and self-examination, declaring, "The unexamined life is not worth living." His method of dialectic questioning, aimed at uncovering truths about ethics and virtue, laid the groundwork for Stoic teachings.

Cynic Influence

Zeno's first teacher was Crates of Thebes, who was a pupil of Diogenes of Sinope (the founder of Cynicism). The Cynics had a significant impact on Zeno and the development of his ideas around philosophy. Cynicism advocated for a life in accordance with nature, rejecting conventional desires for wealth, power, and fame. Diogenes, known for his ascetic lifestyle and disdain for societal norms, influenced the Stoics' value of self-sufficiency and the importance of virtue over material possessions. Diogenes embodied his philosophy by living on the streets and sleeping in a large earthen wine jar, stating, "He has the most who is most content with the least."

Influence of Epicureanism

Although often contrasted with Stoicism, Epicureanism also influenced Stoic thought. Founded by Epicurus, this school emphasized the pursuit of tranquility through the avoidance of pain and fear. While Stoics disagreed with the Epicurean focus on physical pleasure as the highest good, both groups wanted to achieve a state of inner peace and freedom from disturbance and believed people should moderate their desires.

DEVELOPMENT OF STOICISM

Stoicism developed over several crucial periods, including the following.

Early Stoa (300 B.C.E.–150 B.C.E.)

Zeno's teachings were continued by his successors, Cleanthes and Chrysippus, who significantly developed Stoic doctrines. Cleanthes, known for his tribute called "Hymn to Zeus," emphasized the unity of the cosmos and the role of divine reason (*Logos*). Chrysippus, often considered the cofounder of Stoicism, systematized and expanded Stoic philosophy, integrating logic, physics, and ethics into a cohesive framework.

Middle Stoa (150 B.C.E.–C.E. 50)

The Stoic movement evolved further with thinkers like Panaetius and Posidonius, who introduced Stoic ideas to Rome. Panaetius softened some of the harshness of early Stoicism and made it more palatable to Roman sensibilities, teaching the idea that a rational soul is one that directs itself toward goodness and truth. For his part, Posidonius explored the connections between Stoicism and other philosophical traditions, such as Platonism and Aristotelianism.

Late Stoa (C.E. 50–C.E. 200)

The Late Stoa saw Stoicism reach its zenith under Roman philosophers such as Seneca, Epictetus, and Marcus Aurelius. These thinkers adapted Stoicism to address practical and ethical concerns, emphasizing personal improvement and resilience. They are the best known of the Stoic philosophers due to the larger volume of their surviving texts and writings, and the accessibility of their teachings.

THE BIG THREE STOIC PHILOSOPHERS

There were arguably three most important philosophers relating to Stoicism: Seneca, Epictetus, and Marcus Aurelius.

Seneca

A statesman, playwright, and advisor to Emperor Nero, Seneca focused his writings on practical ethics and the pursuit of virtue in daily life. He was a prolific writer, best known for his treatises on anger and time management, as well his philosophical correspondence with his friend Lucilius.

Epictetus

A former enslaved person, Epictetus taught that true freedom comes from within and emphasized the importance of focusing on what is within your control, stating, "It's not what happens to you, but how you react to it that matters." Epictetus was heavily influenced by Socrates and taught through deep questioning of his students. Fortunately, his teachings were well documented by his student Arrian and compiled into the *Enchiridion* and *Discourses of Epictetus*.

Marcus Aurelius

The Roman emperor and philosopher Marcus Aurelius practiced Stoicism to manage the immense responsibilities and pressures of his role. His personal writings, known as his *Meditations*, show a man striving to live a virtuous life while holding a position of enormous power. His self-focused exhortations such as, "Be like the promontory against which the waves continually break; but it stands firm and tames the fury of the water around it," still apply today.

Overall, the Stoic movement, shaped by early influences from Socratic, Cynic, and Epicurean philosophies, evolved through the contributions of many great thinkers over multiple centuries. From its origins in Athens to its development in Rome, Stoicism has remained a powerful guide for living a virtuous and resilient life. By focusing on what is within one's control and cultivating inner peace, Stoic philosophy offers timeless wisdom that continues to resonate in the modern world.

ZENO OF CITIUM

The Founder of Stoicism

Quotable Voices

"The goal of life is living in agreement with nature."

—Zeno of Citium

Zeno of Citium was a wealthy merchant and the founder of the Stoic school of philosophy. He drew influences from Socrates, Plato, and Aristotle, as well as the moral ideas of the Cynics. He lived a spare and simple life in spite of his wealth. He was drawn to philosophy as a practical way to live a good life and maintain peace of mind. Little did he know that his ideas would end up influencing great statesmen such as Cato the Younger, Cicero, and Marcus Aurelius.

EARLY LIFE AND CONVERSION TO PHILOSOPHY

Zeno was born in the Phoenician colony Citium in Cyprus in 334 B.C.E. The philosopher had a Greek name and Greek education, but his ancestry is disputed; scholars are uncertain if he was Phoenician or Greek. Plus, Zeno is also reported to have only spoken Greek, and his father's name, Mnaseas, was a meaningful word in both Greek and Phoenician.

On a voyage from Phoenicia to Peiraeus, Zeno survived a shipwreck and ended up in Athens. While pondering what to do next, Zeno apparently consulted the oracle of Delphi and was instructed that he should seek the same complexion as the dead. He inferred this to mean that he should study the books of the ancients.

Following the advice of the oracle, he often visited a bookstore in Athens. He became interested in philosophy after reading Xenophon's *Memorabilia*, fascinated with its portrayal of Socrates. He approached the bookseller and asked him where he might find someone like Socrates to instruct him. At the same moment, Crates of Thebes, the most famous Cynic in Athens, happened to be walking by. The bookseller pointed to Crates, and Zeno became his student shortly after. Zeno later commented that even though he'd suffered a shipwreck, it was a prosperous journey because of his introduction to philosophy.

PHILOSOPHICAL INFLUENCES

As a student of Crates, Zeno was heavily influenced by the Cynic school of philosophy, which argued that people were rational animals, and that the purpose of life was to live with reason and according to nature. Cynics felt that a person should live according to one's own natural sense of reason by living simply and shamelessly, rejecting social constraints. The Cynics lived spare, ascetic lives, meaning that they rejected wealth, power, worldly possessions, and fame. Crates of Thebes even gave away a large fortune to live in poverty and teach in Athens.

While Zeno studied under Crates, he showed a strong inclination toward learning philosophy, but due to his modesty, he struggled to adopt the Cynics' shamelessness. In an effort to change him, Crates gave Zeno a pot of lentil soup to carry in the streets of Athens. The shy Zeno felt embarrassed carrying an open pot of lentil soup out in public and tried to hide it under his cloak. Upon seeing Zeno's discomfort, Crates broke the pot with his staff. Zeno ran away with lentil soup streaming down his legs, with Crates admonishing him, "Why run away, my little Phoenician? Nothing terrible has befallen you."

The Cynics felt that material goods, wealth, and fame were antithetical to living a good life. However, Zeno conceived the material as "indifferents," meaning that they were neither good nor bad, but that they were things with which you could develop virtue against. In his thirst for knowledge, Zeno studied under the Megarians, the Academics, and the Platonists, merging these philosophies into his own school of thought.

FOUNDING OF THE STOIC SCHOOL

Zeno felt that philosophy should be shared openly and widely among any who wished to learn. In 301 B.C.E., he began teaching his philosophical ideas in the streets of Athens at the Stoa Poikile (Painted Porch), from which Stoicism derives its name. Initially, his followers were called Zenonians but eventually became known as Stoics.

CORE TEACHINGS AND PHILOSOPHY

Like many of the Socratic philosophers, Zeno focused on promoting rational and ethical living as the path to a good life. He adopted Plato's and Aristotle's ideas of virtue (living with wisdom, courage, justice, and temperance) but disagreed with Aristotle's notion that a good life also needed external things such as wealth, health, and beauty. (For more on the topic of virtue, see the Virtue section.)

Zeno taught that there were three fundamental branches of philosophy: logic, physics, and ethics. He believed that logic was necessary to develop wisdom and to avoid being deceived. His idea of physics theorized a universe with a rational, purposeful structure (the *Logos*). But his main focus was on ethics and living a virtuous life, which he felt was the key to true happiness and equanimity.

INFLUENCE AND LEGACY

Very little of Zeno's works have survived, so most of what is known of him and his teachings comes from reports and quotations of other philosophers and historians, most notably from Diogenes Laërtius's *Lives of Eminent Philosophers*. Diogenes Laërtius, commenting on Zeno's character, writes, "Though he was in other respects very energetic in his application to philosophy, still he was too modest for the shamelessness of the Cynics."

Zeno died around 262 B.C.E. The leadership of the Stoic school was taken up by Cleanthes, one of his most ardent students. Zeno's ideas and the spread of Stoicism throughout the Hellenistic world and into Rome made a lasting influence on later philosophical and ethical thought.

SENECA THE YOUNGER

Stoic Philosopher, Statesman, Playwright

Quotable Voices

"Men do not care how nobly they live, but only for how long,
although it is within the reach of every man to live nobly,
but within no man's power to live long."

—Seneca

Lucius Annaeus Seneca the Younger, generally referred to as Seneca, was a philosopher, statesman, and playwright. He was active in politics as a Roman senator and later was an advisor to Emperor Nero. Seneca wrote twelve essays and 124 letters about philosophical and ethical issues throughout his life, contributing greatly to the body of Stoic philosophy and earning him a place as one of the most important Stoic thinkers. Seneca is considered one of the more accessible Stoic writers due to his clear style and excellent prose.

In addition, ten plays are attributed to Seneca, including *Medea*, *Phaedra*, and *Thyestes*. All his plays are dark and grim tragedies, which starkly contrast to his Stoic teachings and writings. Interestingly, his plays were well read throughout medieval and Renaissance Europe, influencing dramatic playwrights of the time, including Shakespeare.

EARLY LIFE

Seneca was born around 4 B.C.E. in Córdoba, Hispania (modern-day Spain). His father was a Spanish-born Roman knight, who was a famous writer and teacher of rhetoric in Rome. Seneca went to Rome around the age of five. As a high-born Roman, he received a well-rounded education including studies in rhetoric, literature, and grammar. Seneca was tutored in philosophy by Attalus the Stoic, whom Seneca mentions often in his writings, holding him in high esteem.

POLITICAL CAREER AND EXILE

Seneca was a successful senator and was well known for his oratory skills. However, in his writings, he referred to Emperor Caligula as a monster. In response, Caligula ordered Seneca to commit suicide, but he was spared when, due to an illness, his friends convinced Caligula that Seneca would die soon anyway. Fortunately for Seneca, Caligula's reign was cut short when he was assassinated in 41 C.E.

Seneca's good fortune didn't last long. While he escaped Caligula's wrath, he was accused of infidelity with Caligula's sister, Julia Livilla, and he was sentenced to death; however, most historians agree that the charges were likely false. The new emperor, Claudius, instead exiled Seneca to Corsica, where Seneca spent the next eight years.

PHILOSOPHICAL WORKS

Seneca was a prolific writer, well known for covering a wide range of topics with keen observations about living according to virtue, wealth, time management, and dealing with grief. For example, in his essay *On the Shortness of Life*, he writes, "It is not that we have a short time to live, but that we waste a lot of it. Life is long enough, and a sufficiently generous amount has been given to us for the highest achievements if it were all well invested."

In his *Moral Letters to Lucilius* (also called *Letters from a Stoic*), which was an ongoing correspondence with his friend, Seneca provides a treasure trove of the practical application of Stoic ideals. For example, he tells Lucilius how to live contently, advising, "No person has the power to have everything they want, but it is in their power not to want what they don't have, and to cheerfully put to good use what they do have."

SENECA AND NERO

Seneca returned to Rome in 49 C.E. when Claudius married Caligula's sister Agrippina, and she persuaded Claudius to cancel Seneca's exile. Upon his return, Seneca was appointed as tutor to Agrippina's son, the future emperor, Nero. When Nero became emperor, Seneca became his advisor, and his guidance ensured that the first five years of Nero's reign were successful and prosperous.

As Nero's behavior became more erratic, Seneca's influence on him waned. Seneca was also caught up in political intrigue and accused of using his office to enrich himself. This may have been true, as Seneca was extremely rich and owned several estates throughout the Roman Empire. Around this time, Seneca wrote *On the Happy Life*, where he claimed that gaining wealth along Stoic lines was proper for a philosopher.

Seneca tried to retire from public office twice but each time was refused by Nero. Unable to curb Nero's excesses and tiring from political intrigue, Seneca spent more time in the countryside focusing on his studies and writing, rarely visiting Rome. It was during this time that he wrote *Natural Questions*, an encyclopedia of the natural world, and the previously mentioned *Moral Letters to Lucilius*.

DEATH

In 65 C.E., Seneca was caught up in the aftermath of the attempted assassination of Nero. Historians argue Seneca's actual involvement, but Nero ordered Seneca to commit suicide. Seneca accepted his fate stoically and with dignity. After dictating his will to a scribe, Seneca, in his home surrounded by friends, cut his wrists. Due to his age and illness, his blood loss was slow and painful, denying him a quick death. He also took poison, but it failed to end his life. Interestingly, Seneca's wife, Pompeia Paulina, also cut her wrists, but Nero ordered she be saved.

LEGACY

Seneca's life and works have had an enduring legacy in philosophy, literature, and political thought. With his practical advice for living virtuously in a turbulent world, his works have had a profound influence on later philosophical and religious thought, including early Christianity and Renaissance Humanism. His teachings continue to offer guidance on ethical living and mental resilience.

SENECA ON TIME MANAGEMENT

Ancient Wisdom for Modern Efficiency

Quotable Voices

"Life is long if you know how to use it."

—Seneca

Seneca was a Roman Stoic philosopher, statesman, and playwright whose wide-ranging works have influenced political and philosophical thinking, the structure of dramatic plays, and grief. Seneca's thoughts on time management are particularly important and are demonstrated in his essay *On the Shortness of Life* and his correspondence published as *Moral Letters to Lucilius*.

You may ask: Why time management? Wouldn't this be a topic better left to planners? Seneca's views on time management aren't just about daily productivity; they are also about developing a mindset about time and how to use it wisely throughout all areas of life. Seneca's time management focuses on understanding what's important and ignoring the rest, so you don't regret your time on Earth.

THE VALUE OF TIME

For Seneca, time was the most valuable resource because it couldn't be renewed. He felt that a person's time should be fiercely guarded, writing, "People are frugal in guarding their personal property; but as soon as it comes to squandering time they are most wasteful of the one thing in which it is right to be stingy."

MISCONCEPTIONS ABOUT TIME

Seneca argued against the belief that one needs more time to live well. He felt that it didn't matter how long a person lives, but rather how well they live with the time they have. Seneca understood that a person doesn't really control the length of their life, and that even if they lived a long life, it did not necessarily mean that they lived a good life.

COMMON TIME-WASTERS

In *On the Shortness of Life*, Seneca gives a list of time-wasters that were not only common in ancient Rome but are also very applicable today. He criticizes those who procrastinate: "Putting things off is the biggest waste of life: it snatches away each day as it comes, and denies us the present by promising the future." He also chastises those who waste time pursuing power or unnecessary indulgences for investing time in the wrong pursuits, writing, "You act like mortals in all that you fear, and like immortals in all that you desire." In summary, Seneca felt that spending time on things that don't align with a virtuous life wasted not only one's time but also one's life.

SENECA'S PRINCIPLES OF TIME MANAGEMENT

Seneca was clear about his feelings toward how a person spent their time. The following are pillars of his preferred way to approach time management.

Setting Clear and Ethical Priorities

Seneca, like other Stoic philosophers, felt that pursuing external statuses such as wealth and power wouldn't offer a happy and fulfilling life. He explains, "Of all people only those are at leisure who make time for philosophy, only those are really alive." Seneca believed only by having philosophy-driven self-awareness and living with virtue can a person's life flourish.

Living in the Present

Seneca urges that living in the present moment is one of the core precepts to managing one's time responsibly, writing, "Everyone hustles his life along, and is troubled by a longing for the future and weariness of the present. But the man who [...] organizes every day as though it were his last, neither longs for nor fears the next day." By acting as if each day is your last, you are able to be more present in your lives and focus on what truly matters.

Avoiding Busyness

Busyness, meaning mistaking activity for progress, is something that Seneca warns against. "There is nothing the busy man is less busied with than living," he penned, advising people to steer clear of being busy at the cost of living a good life. "No one will bring back the years; no one will restore you to yourself," he writes as a warning that busyness only brings a life filled with regret from wasted opportunities.

Prioritize Tasks and Avoid Distractions

Seneca recommends prioritizing tasks according to their true value. By aligning what you do with your values and avoiding distractions, you focus on what really matters. Seneca advises:

> "So, concerning the things we pursue, and for which we vigorously exert our-selves, we owe this consideration—either there is nothing useful in them, or most aren't useful. Some of them are superfluous, while others aren't worth that much. But we don't discern this and see them as free, when they cost us dearly."
>
> —Seneca

Basically, much of what a person thinks is important usually is a waste of time, so focus on things that matter most.

Rejuvenation and Reflection

Seneca was also a proponent of taking time off to relax, reflect, and rejuvenate. In his essay *On Tranquility of Mind*, he writes, "The mind should not be kept continuously at the same pitch of concentration, but given amusing diversions. . . . Our minds must relax." He then advises taking a walk and getting out into nature, taking time away from social settings, and even enjoying wine in moderation.

Seneca's views on time management are not just about being efficient; they are also about enhancing the quality of life. He offers timeless principles and actionable advice for managing one's time in a way that aligns with living a meaningful and ethical life.

EPICTETUS

The Resilient Sage

Epictetus was a Greek philosopher, born around 50 C.E. in Hierapolis, Phrygia (present-day Turkey). He was born enslaved, which shaped his perspectives on freedom and control. His birth name is unknown, as the Greek word *epíktētos* simply means "gained" or "acquired." His teachings on moral ethics and the Dichotomy of Control have profoundly influenced both ancient and modern thought.

Where the high-born Seneca was known for his elegant writing and speaking style, the low-born Epictetus was more direct, frank, and often humorous in his teachings. In speaking about death, he quips, "I have to die. If it is now, well then I die now; if later, then now I will take my lunch, since the hour for lunch has arrived—and dying I will tend to later."

EARLY LIFE

Epictetus spent his early life as an enslaved person in Rome to Epaphroditos, a wealthy former enslaved person and secretary to Nero. Though Epictetus was enslaved, the imperial connection of his master and his education afforded him a higher status than that of a common enslaved person. He was permitted to study Stoic philosophy under a well-respected Stoic, Musonius Rufus.

LATER LIFE

After Epictetus was released from enslavement around 68 C.E., he began to teach philosophy in Rome. In 93 C.E., Emperor Domitian banished all philosophers from Rome because he was wary of their influence on citizens against his dictatorship. So, Epictetus moved to Nicopolis in Greece, where he established his own school of philosophy. He lived a simple life and was alone for most of his life. In his old age, he adopted a friend's child who otherwise may have died and raised him with the help of a woman, though it's unknown if they were married. Epictetus died sometime around 135 C.E.

CORE TEACHINGS AND PHILOSOPHY

Epictetus, like most Stoic philosophers, felt that the beginning of growth was self-examination. He teaches, "It's not what happens to you, but how you react to it that matters." In other words, people should examine how their perspectives of external events and circumstances caused them to make judgments, and how their misjudgments may have caused them distress. By questioning your perceptions (impressions) before you insist (assent) that your perceptions are correct, you make correct judgments more frequently. For more on this subject, see the section on Impressions and Assent.

For Epictetus, understanding what one has control over, namely one's will, is essential to living a good life. Trying to control things outside of your control, like the actions of others, your reputation, and even your body, is futile and causes internal distress and dissatisfaction. He states, "Freedom is the only worthy goal in life. It is won by disregarding things that lie beyond our control." For more on this topic, see The Dichotomy of Control section.

"No man is free who is not master of himself," says Epictetus, teaching his students the importance of self-discipline. He reasons that because one only has control over oneself, that if one did not practice self-discipline, one would have no control in one's life, and therefore would not be free.

WORKS

Epictetus never wrote any of his teachings, preferring to question his students in the style of his hero, Socrates. Though there are no written works by Epictetus, his lectures were transcribed by his pupil Arrian and compiled into two works: *Discourses* and the *Enchiridion*, or Handbook. In the preface to *Discourses*, Arrian writes, "Whatever I heard him say I used to write down, word for word, as best I could, endeavoring to preserve it as a memorial, for my own future use, of his way of thinking and the frankness of his speech."

INFLUENCE AND LEGACY

Emperor Hadrian appreciated Epictetus's teaching and attended some of his lectures in Nicopolis. Hadrian ordered his adopted son Antoninus to adopt a young Marcus Aurelius, who would later be considered one of the greatest emperors to have ever ruled the Roman Empire.

Epictetus influenced other Stoic thinkers and later philosophical and religious movements, including Christianity. Marcus Aurelius mentions his name in *Meditations* as a key influence on his own philosophical thinking. In 1450, the *Enchiridion* was translated by the Renaissance humanist Niccolò Perotti and was popular throughout Europe for the next two centuries.

Like other Stoic philosophers, Epictetus emphasized philosophy as a way of life, not just a theoretical pursuit. His teachings were practical rather than being a formal presentation of Stoic philosophy. With his sharp wit and logical reasoning through examples in daily life, Epictetus made important contributions to Stoic philosophy that have lasted through the ages.

MARCUS AURELIUS

Philosopher Emperor of Rome

Quotable Voices

"Waste no more time arguing about
what a good man should be. Be one."

—Marcus Aurelius

Marcus Aurelius was a Roman emperor and Stoic philosopher. He was considered one of the greatest leaders of Rome because of his ethical leadership and concern for the well-being of those he governed. He was the last of what historians called the Five Good Emperors—a time of relative peace and prosperity within the Roman Empire.

EARLY LIFE

Marcus Aurelius was born in 121 C.E. to a prominent and wealthy family. His father died when he was three, and he was primarily raised by his mother and paternal grandfather. In speaking of his grandfather, he writes in *Meditations*, "From my grandfather Verus I learned good morals and the government of my temper."

Marcus Aurelius was educated at home according to aristocratic traditions of the time. Diognetus, a painting master, introduced Aurelius to philosophy, and, as a result, he took on the sparse dress of a philosopher and slept on the floor until his mother intervened. From this early introduction to philosophy, Aurelius developed his moral center that would guide him through the challenges of being the most powerful man in the world.

In 138 C.E., Emperor Hadrian ordered Antoninus, who was next in the line of succession, to adopt Marcus Aurelius to ensure his accession. Hadrian died later that year, and Aurelius became heir to the throne.

INTRODUCTION TO STOICISM

Aurelius's education continued as he was groomed to become emperor. He received instruction in oratory, law, Greek, and Latin. It was during this time that he was tutored by the Stoic philosophers Rusticus and Apollonius, beginning a lifelong commitment to Stoic principles. He was especially influenced by Rusticus, writing in his *Meditations*, "I am indebted to him [Rusticus] for being acquainted with the discourses of Epictetus, which he communicated to me out of his own collection."

ASCENSION TO POWER AND GOVERNANCE

On the death of Antoninus in 161 C.E., the Senate planned to recognize Marcus Aurelius as emperor, but he refused unless his adopted brother Lucius Verus was also given a title. The Senate accepted, and though the men were given the titles of co-emperor, it was clear that Aurelius was the more senior emperor. Verus served as co-emperor until his death in 169 C.E.

Aurelius's approach to governance was characterized by a commitment to duty and the welfare of his people. He avoided the excesses of previous emperors and often chafed at the extravagances of life as an emperor. He would have preferred a life of studying philosophy and writing, but he recognized his Stoic duty to use his office to serve the greater good.

PARTHIAN WARS

Soon after Aurelius's ascension to emperor, King Vologases IV of Parthia attacked Armenia, a Roman client state, meaning a semi-autonomous region under the protection of Rome. This was the start of the Parthian Wars, which lasted until 166 C.E., when the Roman armies expelled the Parthians and returned to Rome. Seeing the suffering caused by the wars in his empire, Aurelius, practicing the Stoic virtue of justice, created programs for the rehabilitation of the returning soldiers to help integrate them back into Roman society.

ANTONINE PLAGUE

Soldiers returning from the war carried measles or smallpox home, causing an extended and destructive epidemic that finally ended in 180 C.E. A second outbreak occurred nine years later, when it was reported that two thousand Roman people died per day. The total estimated death toll of the plague is around ten million people. Throughout the plague, Aurelius, holding to the Stoic principles of justice and compassion, raised funds for relief of the victims of the plague, even selling some of his own possessions.

PERSONAL CHALLENGES
AND STOIC RESPONSES

Aurelius faced many personal challenges throughout his life. He suffered from multiple illnesses, including an ulcer and chest pains that were thought to have been caused by the stress of his office. He buried most of his fourteen children, with only five of them outliving him. When one of his chief generals, Avidius Cassius, declared himself emperor in 175 C.E., Aurelius's Stoic response to the betrayal was to forgive him, upholding his commitment to Stoic forgiveness and justice. Throughout these hardships, he continued to carry out his duties as emperor with grace and dignity, staying true to his Stoic principles.

MEDITATIONS AND ITS TEACHINGS

Marcus Aurelius's enduring legacy is due in part to his *Meditations*, a personal journal and philosophical work composed during his military campaigns. In it, he writes on the nature of the mind, the practice of reflection, and the acceptance of fate. Many of his chapters are self-focused and reminded him how to live a Stoic life. For example, he writes:

"At dawn, when you have trouble getting out of bed, tell yourself: 'I have to go to work—as a human being. What do I have to complain of, if I'm going to do what I was born for—the things I was brought into the world to do? Or is this what I was created for? To huddle under the blankets and stay warm?—But it's nicer here. So you were born to feel 'nice'? Instead of doing things and experiencing them?'"

—Marcus Aurelius

With this, he forbids himself from letting comfort and pleasure take precedence over doing his duty.

LEGACY AND DEATH

Marcus Aurelius died in 180 C.E. of unknown causes, and his son Commodus was made emperor. Even though Commodus had ruled as co-emperor with his father since 177 C.E., he was erratic and ill prepared to rule. His leadership style became more dictatorial as he got caught up in political intrigue and was assassinated in 192 C.E.

Marcus Aurelius was a shining example of ethical leadership, determination, and a commitment to the Stoic ideal of living a virtuous life. Where previous emperors indulged in excess and debauchery, Aurelius served with restraint, fairness, and compassion that stands as an example of how to wield power for the betterment of humanity.

MARCUS AURELIUS'S
MEDITATIONS

Timeless Wisdom for Personal Reflection

Quotable Voices

"What then is that which is able to conduct a man? One thing and only one, philosophy. But this consists in keeping the daemon within a man free from violence and unharmed, superior to pains and pleasures, doing nothing without purpose, nor yet falsely and with hypocrisy."

—Marcus Aurelius

Marcus Aurelius, the Roman emperor from 161 to 180 C.E., is often remembered not only for his leadership but also for his profound philosophical writings. Aurelius's *Meditations* stands as a monumental text of Stoic philosophy, offering insights into human nature, ethics, and the pursuit of wisdom. Written as a series of personal reflections rather than a glorification of his achievements and conquests, *Meditations* provides a window into the mind of one of history's most powerful leaders and showcases the enduring relevance of Stoic principles.

HISTORICAL CONTEXT

Marcus Aurelius wrote *Meditations* during his military campaigns between 170 and 180 C.E. Despite his position as emperor of Rome, he faced numerous challenges, including wars, political intrigue, and personal loss. It was against this backdrop that he penned his thoughts, initially intended for his own guidance and self-improvement.

THE STRUCTURE AND CONTENT

Meditations is divided into twelve books, each composed of various reflections, aphorisms, and personal notes. The text lacks a formal structure, as it was not intended for publication. Instead, it served as a diary where Aurelius grappled with his thoughts and sought to align his actions with his Stoic beliefs.

CENTRAL THEMES OF *MEDITATIONS*

Throughout the text, Aurelius addresses the following important themes.

Gratitude and Friendship

Even as emperor, Aurelius continually strove for self-improvement and to live up to his Stoic ideals. He looked to those who could help him become his ideal self. He begins *Meditations* by thanking those who impacted his life and listing what he learned from them.

Impermanence and Mortality

Aurelius frequently reflected on the transient nature of life and urged himself to make the most of his time by living virtuously. "You could leave life right now. Let that determine what you do and say and think," he writes, as a reminder to himself of the importance of living each day according to his values and principles.

Rationality and Virtue

As a Stoic, Aurelius emphasized living in accordance with reason and virtue, considering these the highest goods. Even in his position as emperor he sought to improve: "If a thing is difficult to be accomplished by thyself, do not think that it is impossible for man: but if anything is possible for man and conformable to his nature, think that this can be attained by thyself too." He remained open to criticism from others, willing to change his thinking and behavior when exposed to the truth. He found a bruised ego less painful than remaining ignorant.

Inner Peace and Self-Control

Aurelius writes about maintaining tranquility and controlling one's emotions, regardless of the circumstances, reminding himself, "You have power over your mind—not outside events. Realize this, and you will find strength." Aurelius constantly reminded himself to keep his mind clear and calm to avoid being overwhelmed from the many pressures of ruling an empire.

Interconnectedness and Duty

Marcus Aurelius often reflected on the social nature of humans and the importance of fulfilling one's role in society with integrity, stating, "For whatsoever either by myself or with another I can do, ought to be directed to this only, to that which is useful and well suited to society." As emperor, Aurelius felt it was his duty to be an example of Stoic virtue and to continually encourage others to live up to their better natures.

STOIC PRINCIPLES IN *MEDITATIONS*

Meditations also includes the following principles inherent to Stoicism.

The Dichotomy of Control

One of the core Stoic teachings present in *Meditations* is the Dichotomy of Control, which distinguishes between what a person can and cannot control. In numerous passages, Aurelius reminds himself to focus on his actions and attitudes, rather than external events.

Acceptance of Fate (*Amor Fati*)

Marcus Aurelius encourages others to embrace their fate and to always practice virtue when he says, "Accept the things to which fate binds you, and love the people with whom fate brings you together, but do so with all your heart."

Reflective Practice

The Stoics emphasized taking time for self-reflection as a means for improving oneself. The very act of writing *Meditations* was a form of reflective practice, a method for Aurelius to align his thoughts and actions with Stoic philosophy.

IMPACT AND LEGACY

Meditations has had a lasting impact on both ancient and modern thought. Its influence extends beyond philosophy into areas such as psychology, leadership, and personal development. The text offers practical advice that remains relevant today, particularly in its emphasis on resilience, mindfulness, and ethical living.

MODERN RELEVANCE

Many contemporary leaders draw inspiration from Marcus Aurelius's emphasis on duty, humility, and self-discipline. *Meditations* continues to be a source of guidance and inspiration, offering a profound look into the mind of a philosopher-king who sought to live by the principles he cherished.

Aurelius's *Meditations* stands as a testament to the enduring power of Stoic philosophy. Through his personal reflections, Aurelius provides timeless wisdom on living a virtuous and meaningful life. His writings emphasize that even in the face of immense responsibility and adversity, one can find inner peace and strength through rationality, self-control, and a commitment to the common good. As you navigate the complexities of modern life, Marcus Aurelius's reflections serve as a beacon, guiding you toward a life of virtue, resilience, and inner tranquility.

THE DICHOTOMY OF CONTROL

Understanding What You Have Power Over

Quotable Voices

"Some things are within our power, while others are not.
Within our power are opinion, motivation, desire, aversion, and,
in a word, whatever is of our own doing; not within our power
are our body, our property, reputation, office, and, in a word,
whatever is not of our own doing."

—Epictetus

In the heart of Stoicism lies a simple yet transformative concept: the Dichotomy of Control. This simple principle can change the way you view your life and the world around you, and offer clarity in the midst of chaos. Stoicism advocates learning to distinguish what is in one's control and what is not, leading to a more fulfilling, less anxious life. Think of it as the original version of "Don't sweat the small stuff. And it's all small stuff."

THE CONCEPT OF WILL

The Stoics held a clear and practical view on the nature of control, emphasizing the distinction between what is and isn't within one's power. Central to their philosophy is the concept of the will, which they argued is the domain over which individuals have absolute control. According to Stoicism, the only things within one's realm of control are functions of the mind that one can govern through reason and self-discipline, which includes the following.

Perceptions

The Stoics felt the key to self-control was to be aware of one's perceptions and how they influence one's thinking in any situation. Your perception is the driver of your decisions and actions. This idea was so important
to the Stoics that they encouraged examining one's impressions (what
one thinks or senses) before one assents (agrees) to the impression.

Decisions

The Stoics also thought that the ability to rationally think through
the decisions that one makes is very much under one's control. A person always can make a choice in any situation, regardless of whether
or not they like the options available to them.

The Stoics held that each person has control over their actions.
How one chooses to conduct oneself in any situation is a matter of
will. By using one's ability for rational thinking, a person can take
actions that help them live a virtuous life.

Attitudes

The Stoics also believed that a person's feelings about any situation are under their own control. Epictetus, one the most prominent
Stoics, once said, "It is in your power to be happy while you are suffering what you suffer." A Stoic could be in the direst of circumstances
and still choose their attitude because their internal perspective
supersedes any external circumstances.

EXTERNALS

On the other hand, there are countless things that a person has no control over—the weather, the actions of others, the passage of time, and

the stock market's whims—all things that the Stoics would consider as Externals.

Philosophical Definition

Externals: Anything that is outside of one's control, or will, is considered an External. Externals are not considered good or bad, but rather neutral things that are challenges whereupon a person can cultivate virtue.

Why did the Stoics view the distinction between what one can and can't control to be so crucial? They believed when one understands and focuses on what they can control, one maximizes their effectiveness while maintaining their inner calm. Trying to control things that are outside of one's control creates unnecessary stress and disappointment and wastes time and energy.

Imagine you're preparing for an important presentation. You can control how well prepared you are by doing the appropriate research, crafting your message, and rehearsing. What you can't control are technical glitches that might occur or whether your audience likes your presentation. A Stoic approach is to do your best and to let the chips fall where they may, without any attachment to the outcome.

A CALL TO ACTION

Even with no control over outside influences, however, a person should not fall into passivity or indifference. Quite the opposite—they must actively engage with what is within their realm of influence with a serene detachment from outcomes. When a Stoic steps up and acts where they can, it doesn't matter what life throws their way. It's about doing their duty, playing their part well, and then stepping back, knowing the result will be what it will be.

The Stoics argued that recognizing and accepting these limits is not a form of resignation but a path to freedom. Life is full of challenges, and circumstances are not always in one's favor. A person may not always like the available choices they have, but when they fail to act on the things they do have control over, they are at the mercy of external circumstances and allow themself to become a victim. By recognizing what they can control, taking action, and letting go of what they cannot control, a Stoic increases their chance of success while maintaining their inner peace, knowing that they did what they could.

Applying this principle in daily life requires practice and mindfulness. It starts with small moments, like choosing not to get frustrated in traffic, and builds to more significant challenges, such as navigating personal loss or professional setbacks. The goal isn't to become emotionless or to stop caring about the world around you. It's about finding that sweet spot to face life's curveballs with a cool head and a heart ready to tackle what one can actually change. The key is to consistently ask yourself: "Is this within my control?" If the answer is no, a Stoic learns to release their grip and find peace in the acceptance of what is.

In essence, the Dichotomy of Control offers a Stoic compass for navigating life's uncertainties and challenges. It teaches one to focus on one's own actions and attitudes, to engage fully with what one can change, and to release any attachment to outcomes. It's a reminder that, while you can't control the wind, you can adjust your sails, navigate through life's storms, and maybe even enjoy the ride.

APPLYING THE DICHOTOMY OF CONTROL IN EVERYDAY LIFE

How to Be More Productive and Peaceful

Stoic philosophy offers many tools that can enhance your daily life, one of which is the Dichotomy of Control. This concept, vividly articulated by the Stoic philosopher Epictetus, helps people understand what is and isn't within their control. Understanding and applying this distinction can lead to a more serene and effective approach to life. So, read on to explore how it applies to daily life.

UNDERSTANDING THE DICHOTOMY OF CONTROL

In the simplest terms, Stoicism teaches that all a person has control over is one's own thinking, choices, and actions. Everything else is outside of their direct control. A person can influence things by their choices and actions, but that is all. This foundational idea teaches that a person's emotional and mental well-being hinge on focusing one's efforts only on those things one can control and letting go of what one cannot control.

PRACTICAL APPLICATIONS

The Dichotomy of Control can be applied to many day-to-day scenarios, including the following.

Career and Work

In the workplace, it's easy to feel frustrated by delayed projects, difficult colleagues, or decisions by upper management. Here, applying the Dichotomy of Control means focusing on your response and your work ethic rather than external outcomes. You can control how you react to feedback, the quality of your work, and how you communicate with others. However, decisions like who gets promoted or how colleagues behave are outside of your direct control. When someone is properly grounded in life, they shouldn't have to look outside themselves for approval. As Epictetus suggests, "Make the best use of what is in your power, and take the rest as it happens."

Health and Fitness

When it comes to health, you can control your diet, exercise, and sleep habits, but not the genetic limitations of your body or the unexpected onset of a disease. A Stoic approach would be to focus on your fitness regimen and diet without becoming overly attached to specific outcomes like losing a certain amount of weight or gaining a certain amount of muscle within a certain time frame. You can only control how much effort you put in, doing the right exercises, and eating well.

Personal Relationships

While you can strive to be understanding, supportive, and present in your relationships, the feelings and actions of others are outside your control. Stoicism teaches us to accept people as they are, respond with compassion, and not be upset by their reactions. In the words of Epictetus, "Men are disturbed, not by things, but by the principles and notions which they form concerning things." By remembering that what others do and say is outside of your control, you can focus your efforts on how you show up in relationships, leading to healthier interactions and inner calm.

Facing Death

"I cannot escape death, but at least I can escape the fear of it," says Epictetus, stressing that while your life isn't under your control, how you respond to the challenges of life, and eventually your death, is. By learning how to be comfortable with the things you can't control, you can face life and death with calm and grace.

BENEFITS OF EMBRACING THE DICHOTOMY OF CONTROL

The Dichotomy of Control can be useful in many practical ways, including the following.

Reduced Anxiety and Stress

By understanding what you can influence, you reduce unnecessary stress about uncontrollable outcomes, leading to a calmer mind and a more balanced life. You're able to worry less about the things that are outside of your control and do your best to accept the things that life brings your way.

Increased Productivity

When you can recognize what you truly have control over, namely your choices and actions, you can focus on areas where you can influence the outcome. Your efforts are more impactful, because rather than trying to control others or external circumstances, you focus on your own choices.

Improved Relationships

Accepting that you cannot control others but only your responses to them can transform your personal and professional relationships. You're better able to accept others for who they are, without trying to change them, recognizing that it is not in your power to do so. As Marcus Aurelius advises, "Recall to thy mind this conclusion, that rational animals exist for one another, and that to endure is a part of justice, and that men do wrong involuntarily."

The Stoic Dichotomy of Control is not just a philosophical concept; it is also a practical tool that can profoundly impact your daily life. By clearly understanding and applying this principle, you can enhance your mental well-being, productivity, and relationships. As Epictetus aptly notes, "The more we value things outside our control, the less control we have." Embracing what you can change, and accepting what you cannot, makes for a more productive and peaceful life.

VIRTUE

The Sole Good

Quotable Voices

"Of things some are good, some are bad, and others are indifferent. The good then are the virtues and the things which partake of the virtues: the bad are the vices, and the things which partake of them; and the indifferent are the things which lie between the virtues and the vices: wealth, health, life, death, pleasure, pain."

—Epictetus

Unlike many other philosophical traditions, Stoicism teaches that virtue is not merely an attribute of a person's character; it is the very essence of what it takes to live a good life. The Stoics went so far as to posit that living a life of virtue is not just a means to an end but the end itself—the sole good.

Philosophical Definition

virtue: According to the Stoics, virtue is the highest good and consists of living in accordance with reason and nature. Virtue is the foundation of moral character and the key to true happiness. The Stoics held that there are four cardinal virtues: wisdom (the knowledge of what is good and bad), courage (the ability to face fear and adversity with strength), justice (treating others fairly and acting with moral integrity), and temperance (self-control and moderation in all aspects of life).

WHY VIRTUE?

So why would the Stoics argue that the only good in life is the cultivation of virtue? Wouldn't being comfortable, wealthy, or famous also lead to a good life? The reason that the Stoics felt that virtue was the only good is because developing one's virtue is something that is fully under one's control. Things that are external to you are all things outside of your control. Marcus Aurelius, the Roman emperor and Stoic philosopher, succinctly encapsulates this ethos in his *Meditations*: "Very little is needed to make a happy life; it is all within yourself, in your way of thinking."

CONTRAST WITH ARISTOTLE'S VIEW OF VIRTUE

Zeno of Citium, the founder of Stoicism, adopted Plato and Aristotle's idea of the four cardinal virtues as essential for *eudaimonia* (flourishing or happiness). But the Stoics diverged significantly from Aristotle's conception of the good life and the role of virtue within it.

Aristotle felt that virtue, while central to his teachings, is not the sole good; rather, it is part of a broader conception of the good life that includes external goods such as wealth, health, and beauty. Aristotle argued that these external goods, while not intrinsically valuable, contribute to a flourishing life when combined with virtuous activity.

The Stoics, on the other hand, argued that external factors—wealth, health, and even life itself—are indifferent to one's moral character and, therefore, irrelevant to one's happiness. They neither contribute to nor detract from the moral value of your life but are things against which you can improve your virtue. By developing your ability to live virtuously, you can be impervious to the swings of fortune and find inner tranquility in any situation. Epictetus sums it up succinctly when he says, "Show me a man who is sick and happy, in danger and happy, dying and happy, in exile and happy, in disgrace and happy. Show him: I desire, by the gods, to see a Stoic."

WHY THESE VIRTUES?

So why did the Stoics choose these four virtues over all others? For the Stoics, the four cardinal virtues were not just abstract ideals but practical guides for daily conduct and the foundation of ethical living. They help people to manage what is truly within their control—their responses, decisions, and attitudes—thereby fostering resilience, equanimity, and moral clarity, leading to a life that is impervious to external circumstances. Marcus Aurelius explains this in *Meditations* where he writes: "Take me and cast me where thou wilt; for there I shall keep my divine part tranquil, that is, content, if it can feel and act conformably to its proper constitution."

SELF-REINFORCING

The four cardinal virtues are also self-reinforcing. It takes courage to practice the self-awareness needed to develop wisdom. It takes wisdom and temperance to know how to be courageous without being reckless or cowardly. It takes wisdom, courage, and temperance to apply justice fairly without regard to status or wealth. Each virtue is necessary to help you develop and strengthen your other virtues.

IMPLICATIONS OF THE STOIC PERSPECTIVE

The Stoic perspective on virtue as the sole good has profound implications for ethical living. It holds that true contentment and moral excellence lie in one's character and choices, rather than in the accumulation of external goods or the avoidance of discomfort. Epictetus says, "Is freedom anything else than the power of living as we choose? 'Nothing else.'" By cultivating a life of virtue, a person strengthens their character, which in turn helps them to weather the ups and downs of life.

By developing virtue, a person can maintain their integrity in all circumstances, not only those that seem to be negative but those that one might consider positive. History is filled with stories of those who gained wealth, power, or fame, and yet ended up squandering their wealth, abusing their power, or finding themselves destitute because of their lack of character. It takes virtue not only to handle failures but also to manage the pitfalls that can come with success.

Stoicism presents a rigorous and transformative vision of the good life, centered on the primacy of virtue. By positing virtue as the sole good, Stoicism offers a stark contrast to what people often believe contributes to a good life. As you navigate the complexities of modern life, the Stoic commitment to virtue as the sole good remains a powerful beacon, guiding you toward integrity, purpose, and peace.

WISDOM

Understanding the World

To live a good life, the Stoics believed that a person needs to be wise. Not the kind of wise that comes from knowing the capital of every country or being able to recite pi to a hundred digits, but the deep, practical wisdom that helps in navigating life's twists and turns.

So what is Stoic wisdom all about? The Stoics held that because humans are rational animals by nature, they should use this rationality to understand how to act in life. Wisdom isn't just about gaining knowledge; it is also about how to apply that knowledge internally to increase virtue, and externally to help you understand how the world works; this way you can make better choices and contribute to society as a whole.

WISDOM AS A PILLAR

Wisdom is an important pillar in the four virtues of Stoicism. For example, it takes wisdom to know how to practice temperance in life to avoid the opposite extremes of lying on the couch all day watching TV or overworking oneself to the point of burnout. The wiser a person is, the more likely they are to act justly and treat those around them fairly. It's through the application of wisdom that a person knows how to be courageous without being foolhardy or cowardly.

DEVELOPING WISDOM

Stoicism is a practical philosophy, and, while the Stoics felt that knowledge and education were important and necessary for building the foundations of wisdom, they held that a person cultivates wisdom by internal reflection and interactions with the world.

Student of Life

Seneca wrote to Lucilius, "As long as you live, keep learning how to live," as a reminder that a person should be continually developing their own wisdom by being a student of life. The Stoics valued observation, learning, and being curious about the world and people around them. They advised people to watch, listen, and reflect, not just on the nature of the world but also on the nature of one's responses to it.

Understanding What You Control

Developing wisdom, then, is also about honing the ability to distinguish between what you can and cannot control and acting with virtue in those areas you can influence. This is known as the Dichotomy of Control (described in the section The Dichotomy of Control). The Stoics saw wisdom as the pilot of the soul, guiding one through life's storms with the grace of a seasoned captain. It's about asking, "Will freaking out help the situation?" and if the answer is "No," then maybe trying a different approach will help.

Marcus Aurelius writes, "The happiness of those who want to be popular depends on others; the happiness of those who seek pleasure fluctuates with moods outside their control; but the happiness of the wise grows out of their own free acts." His argument is that wisdom is knowing where your real power lies, and it's not in becoming popular or seeking pleasure. It's in managing your own mind and actions.

Our Fellow Humans

Another way to develop wisdom, according to the Stoics, is through engagement with community and society. They understood that humans are social creatures and that much of what you learn about yourself and the world comes through interactions with others. Marcus Aurelius muses, "For it is no way right to be offended with men, but it is thy duty to care for them and to bear with them gently." This suggests that wisdom involves not only personal growth and understanding but also patience and tolerance as you navigate your relationships with others.

Good, Bad, and Indifferent

Wisdom, for the Stoics, also meant understanding the difference among good, bad, and indifferent things. The only true goods were virtues like wisdom itself, while everything else (wealth, health, status) was considered "indifferent"—nice to have, but not essential for a good life. By focusing on developing your character rather than on external things, this perspective helps in managing desires and fears, leading to a more balanced and contented life.

Keeping Perspective

Stoic wisdom is also about seeing the big picture. A Stoic does their best to deal with the situation at hand with rationality and composure, keeping their cool in the face of life's ups and downs, and making choices that align with their deepest values. At the same time, they also keep in mind that while something may feel like a big deal in the moment, it will pass and may even be forgotten in a few weeks or months. It's a kind of inner compass that helps you navigate life's complexities, making sure you keep moving toward what truly matters.

The Stoic approach to wisdom isn't about being the smartest person in the room. It's about being the most centered, the one who knows what matters and what doesn't, and who understands the art of living well. It's a reminder that, in the end, the wisest choice one can make is to focus on being good humans, both for oneself and to others. And maybe, just maybe, that's the secret to navigating life with a little more grace and a lot more peace.

COURAGE

Facing Adversity with Strength

Quotable Voices

"It is not because things are difficult that we do not dare; it is because we do not dare that things are difficult."

—Seneca

Courage is the second pillar in the Stoics' four virtues and occupies a pivotal role in Stoic philosophy's framework for living a virtuous and fulfilling life. Unlike a common definition of courage as bravery in the face of danger, the Stoics broadened this definition to encompass psychological and moral resilience and the fortitude to face not only external challenges but also internal conflicts and adversity.

The Stoics asserted that living according to nature and reason leads to virtue and a flourishing life. Since the Stoics believed the essence of human nature is rational and social, courage in the Stoic sense means that a person should develop the strength to uphold their rational and moral principles even in the face of discomfort, social pressures, or even physical threats. In other words, you must have the courage to stand up for what is right according to reason, rather than what is quick or easy.

RATIONALITY AND COURAGE

Because the Stoics held rationality as a core part of human nature, they posited that when a person practices rationality, it becomes easier to be courageous. Oftentimes the things that you fear are things that cannot actually harm you. By rationally looking at any situation, you can recognize that much of your fear simply comes from your perspective. With that rationality, you gain the courage to do the right things, even if you think that others would not approve. Epictetus touches on this when he says, "When you do anything from a clear judgment that it ought to be done, never shrink from being seen to do it, even though the world should misunderstand it; for if you are not acting rightly, shun the action itself; if you are, why fear those who wrongly censure you?"

THE IMPACT OF COURAGE ON THE OTHER VIRTUES

Courage is the engine that drives the development of the other virtues. It is the attribute that helps put the other virtues into action. Virtues are not cultivated in isolation but rather through courageously engaging with the world.

Justice

Stoicism posits that courage is a necessary component of justice. The Stoic definition of justice is about how one treats other people, and the Stoics believed that one should treat others fairly, regardless of their station in life. One should also have the courage to stand up for justice even if it is challenging or unpopular. As Marcus Aurelius reminds himself, it is important "just that you do the right thing. The rest doesn't matter."

Wisdom

The Stoics believed that a person must actively acknowledge and challenge their perceptions and judgments to gain wisdom. Rather than simply accepting their perception as the truth, a Stoic has the courage to rationally examine their perspectives and be open to other possibilities. Marcus Aurelius highlights the proactive approach of Stoic courage when he writes, "Judge every word and deed which are according to nature to be fit for thee; and be not diverted by the blame which follows from any people nor by their words, but if a thing is good to be done or said, do not consider it unworthy of thee."

Temperance

Practicing Stoic courage means that you have the strength to cultivate temperance and develop the self-discipline to uphold the commitments you make to yourself and others. It takes courage to make choices that benefit yourself and others in the long run, and not give in to excess or laziness. Seneca notes the importance of internalizing courage in regard to temperance when he says, "He is most powerful who governs himself."

RESILIENCE

Stoic courage is not just about overcoming fear; it also extends to developing the resilience to grow from the hardships and challenges of life. Rather than becoming bitter, depressed, or angry, the Stoics celebrated having the courage to embrace life's challenges, transforming them into opportunities for personal growth and the practice of virtue. As Seneca observes, "No man is more unhappy than he who never faces adversity. For he is not permitted to prove himself."

After all, while you may not control external events, you have the power to control your responses and to forge a life of integrity and purpose.

ACCEPTANCE

Another important aspect of Stoic courage is accepting what one cannot change. Far from being apathetic, courageous acceptance of what is outside of your control allows you to focus on what is within your control and use your time and energy where you can be most effective. For example, you might be afraid of what others think or say about you, but remembering that you can't control their opinions allows you to focus on your choices and actions.

The Stoic virtue of courage is a multifaceted and profound aspect of Stoic philosophy. It calls for a deeper engagement with one's values and actions, cultivating a courage that is introspective, ethical, and aligned with the greater good. It is through developing courage that you have the strength to live in accordance with reason, to face adversity with resilience, and to uphold moral principles in the face of personal and external challenges.

JUSTICE

Living with Fairness and Kindness

Quotable Voices
"Live out your life in truth and justice, tolerant of
those who are neither true nor just."
—Marcus Aurelius

In the pantheon of Stoic virtues, justice holds a place of honor, standing alongside wisdom, courage, and temperance as one of the cardinal pillars upon which Stoicism is built. Far from being a mere abstract principle, Stoic justice is a practical guide for living with fairness and kindness. Stoic justice encompasses the ethics of interpersonal relationships and the moral obligation to contribute positively to society.

CULMINATION OF VIRTUES

For the Stoics, justice is the culmination of living with wisdom, courage, and temperance. When a person lives a life of virtue, they have the wisdom and rationality to understand how to treat others fairly, the courage to stand by those principles, and the temperance to use their position for the greater good over personal gain.

TREATMENT OF OTHERS

Justice isn't limited to legal or political frameworks; it's a person's duty to act correctly in all matters, treating others with fairness, respect, and empathy. Marcus Aurelius succinctly captures this ethos in his *Meditations*: "In whatever I do, either by myself or with another, I must direct my energies to this alone, that it shall conduce to the common interest and be in harmony with it." This reflects the Stoic belief in interconnectedness within a community and the importance of contributing to the common good.

Kindness

Seneca emphasized the role of kindness and benevolence as components of justice. "Wherever there is a human being, there is an opportunity for kindness," he writes, suggesting that acts of kindness are both moral duties and opportunities to develop your character and virtue. For Seneca, justice entailed an active engagement with the world, an effort to alleviate suffering, and a commitment to do what is right, even when it is not easy.

Fairness

The Stoic concept of justice also involves fairness in judgment and action. Epictetus advised his students, "Nothing is superior to magnanimity, and gentleness, and love of mankind, and beneficence." Because a person can be easily swayed by their own perceptions, practicing Stoic justice requires you to compassionately look beyond your perceptions to understand and acknowledge the struggles of those around you.

The Stoics held justice as one of the four virtues because the world is not inherently fair. They acknowledged that those who had power often used it to benefit themselves (regardless of its impact on others), and that justice is something that must be advocated for and practiced. A Stoic must take an active role in moving society toward justice by their own personal conduct, as well as by taking a role in civic life.

Wisdom

The Stoics also felt that rationality and wisdom play a key role in the application of justice. Seneca writes, "He who decides a case without hearing the other side, though he decides justly, cannot be considered just." Even if justice is done, if it is done without fully understanding the issue, then it was luck, not justice, that prevailed. A Stoic needs to practice wisdom to help ensure that they are consistent and equal in their judgments and actions.

JUSTICE IN PUBLIC LIFE

Many Stoic philosophers preached the virtues of justice and practiced them in their lives. Cato the Younger, a Roman statesman known for his unwavering integrity, became a symbol of Stoic virtue in his opposition to the corruption and tyranny of Julius Caesar. Cato's life exemplified the Stoic commitment to justice. He demonstrated moral courage and an unyielding adherence to principle, even in the face of personal risk.

Another example is Marcus Aurelius himself, who, despite his immense power as emperor, strove to rule with equity and compassion. His reign is noted for his attempts to make the legal system more equitable for enslaved people and to improve the welfare of the general population. His personal writings reflect a deep engagement with the concept of justice, not only as a ruler but in his personal conduct and relationships as well.

Applying Stoic justice in modern times might mean advocating for policies that promote equity and sustainability, engaging in acts of kindness and service, or simply striving to be fair and understanding in your daily interactions. It challenges everyone to consider the impact of their actions on others and the world, encouraging them to live in a way that contributes to the well-being of all.

Marcus Aurelius, capturing the essence of Stoic justice, writes:

"He who acts unjustly acts impiously. For since the universal nature has made rational animals for the sake of one another to help one another according to their deserts, but in no way to injure one another, he who transgresses her will, is clearly guilty of impiety toward the highest divinity."

—Marcus Aurelius

Marcus Aurelius urged his followers to educate, serve, and be patient with one another in order to form a more just and compassionate world. The Stoic virtue of justice is a call to live with fairness and kindness, to contribute positively to the lives of others, and to strive for a more equitable world. It reminds people that justice is not a distant ideal but a practical guide for daily living, rooted in the recognition of a shared humanity and the interconnectedness of people's lives.

TEMPERANCE

Mastering Desires and Emotions

Quotable Voices
"Most powerful is he who has himself in his own power."

—Seneca

Life is full of distractions and temptations. From the allure of the next shiny gadget to the call of that extra slice of cake, mastering your desires and emotions often seems like a Herculean task. Yet, the timeless wisdom of the Stoics introduces a virtue that feels particularly relevant today: temperance. It's about finding balance in all aspects of life, from your appetites to your emotions. Temperance, an often-overlooked virtue, is the key to living an equanimous and fulfilling life.

Temperance, or moderation, is about self-control. It's the ability to govern your desires and impulses, ensuring they don't drive you toward excess. The Stoics didn't advocate for a joyless existence or deny the pleasures of life. Instead, they taught enjoying life's offerings in moderation, recognizing that overindulgence often leads to dissatisfaction. As Seneca elegantly puts it, "It is not the man who has too little, but the man who craves more, that is poor." True contentment comes not from amassing external goods but from cultivating inner character and restraint.

DICHOTOMY OF CONTROL

Temperance is the cornerstone of the Stoics' Dichotomy of Control. Temperance is vital to practicing discipline over the things that you can control: your perspective, choices, and actions. It also means that you can let go of external, uncontrollable things, such as the actions of others and your reputation.

TEMPERANCE AND THE OTHER VIRTUES

Temperance is vital to the cultivation of the other Stoic virtues. With regard to courage, temperance is what helps a person avoid being reckless or cowardly. Temperance, when applied to justice, is how one achieves balance and fairness in the treatment of others. When it comes to wisdom, temperance helps with practicing self-awareness and having the discipline to question one's assumptions and perspectives.

EMOTIONS

The Stoics felt that temperance is key to managing emotions. Implementing temperance in your life doesn't mean living in a state of perpetual denial or emotional suppression. On the contrary, it's about experiencing life fully and deeply but with a wise moderation that ensures your long-term well-being and happiness. It teaches people to savor the moment, appreciate what they have, and find contentment in simplicity.

MENTAL DISCIPLINE

The Stoics believed that temperance is not just about moderating physical appetites; it extends to one's emotional and mental lives as well. Temperance helps people to maintain a balanced state of mind, even in the face of life's highs and lows. Marcus Aurelius writes, "It is necessary to remember that the attention given to everything has its proper value and proportion. For you will not be dissatisfied if you apply yourself to smaller matters no further than is fit." This passage underlines the importance of temperance in your reactions and emotions. By not allowing external events to disturb your inner equilibrium, you can maintain a sense of composure and act according to virtue, regardless of the circumstances.

MINDFULNESS

Practicing temperance means being mindful of your desires and impulses and asking yourself whether your desires are necessary and beneficial or merely fleeting cravings. Seneca advises, "A consciousness of wrongdoing is the first step to salvation. For a person who is not aware that he is doing anything wrong has no desire to be put right. You have to catch yourself doing it before you can reform." This process of self-reflection is crucial for temperance, as it helps you align your actions with your values and goals, steering clear of mindless indulgence.

LIFE IN BALANCE

Temperance also involves creating a balanced lifestyle that prioritizes what truly matters. It's about finding harmony between work and rest, indulgence and restraint, passion and reason. In doing so, you can lead a richer, more meaningful life. As Marcus Aurelius muses, "Be tolerant with others and strict with yourself." In a world that often celebrates excess, choosing temperance and balance can be a powerful act of defiance and self-empowerment.

START SMALL

But how can you cultivate temperance in a modern world that constantly pushes you toward excess and extravagance and frowns on moderation and restraint? The Stoics recommended that people implement temperance in their lives by starting with small things and moving up to hard challenges. Epictetus advises, "We should discipline ourselves in small things, and from there progress to things of greater value." Forgoing dessert, waking up early, or pausing before sending an angry text are small exercises you can do to develop more discipline in your life.

VOLUNTARY DISCOMFORT

The Stoic practice of voluntary discomfort can also be a valuable tool in your practice of temperance. Seneca advises, "Set aside a certain number of days, during which you shall be content with the scantiest and cheapest fare, with coarse and rough dress, saying to yourself the while: 'Is this the condition that I feared?'" By actively choosing to practice discomfort, a person strengthens their willpower and reminds themself that they can control their desires, rather than being controlled by those desires. Such practices build resilience and enhance one's appreciation for life's simple joys.

Temperance offers a path to mastering your desires and emotions in a world that often feels overwhelming. By practicing self-control, reflection, and moderation, you can navigate life's challenges with grace. Temperance doesn't just make for better individuals; it makes better members of society, contributing to a more balanced and harmonious world. So, the next time you're faced with temptation or turmoil, remember the Stoic wisdom of temperance. In mastering your desires and emotions, you find true freedom and joy.

CHARACTER

Cultivation of Virtue

Quotable Voices

"Such as are your habitual thoughts, such also will be the character of your mind; for the soul is dyed by the thoughts. Dye it then with a continuous series of such thoughts as these: for instance, that where a man can live, there he can also live well."

—Marcus Aurelius

In Stoicism, the cultivation of character is not merely a personal endeavor; it is also a universal imperative aimed at achieving *eudaimonia*, or a flourishing life. Stoics believed that virtue—the excellence of character—is the sole good and that all other "goods" such as wealth, health, and pleasure are "indifferent," neither good nor bad but circumstances where a person can practice virtue. This philosophical stance offers a powerful framework for understanding the true value of character and its impact on the world.

THE FOUNDATION OF STOIC VIRTUE

For the Stoics, living a life of virtue meant aligning one's actions with four cardinal virtues: wisdom, courage, justice, and temperance. These virtues encapsulate the Stoic ideal of living according to reason, which they regarded as the fundamental nature of the universe. Seneca, one of the leading Stoic philosophers, succinctly states, "This, I say, is the highest duty and the highest proof of wisdom—that deed and word should be in accord, that a man should be equal to himself under all conditions, and always the same." The Stoics emphasized self-consistency and integrity as pivotal in the Stoic pursuit of virtue.

Wisdom is the knowledge of right and wrong, courage is the will to act justly even when afraid, justice directs you to act fairly and benevolently toward others, and temperance demands mastery of desires and impulses. These virtues are interdependent, guiding Stoics in every action and decision. (For more on virtue, see the earlier Virtue section.)

EUDAIMONIA: THE STOIC GOAL

The ultimate goal for Stoics is *eudaimonia*, often translated as "happiness" or "flourishing." Unlike the typical definition of happiness as pleasure or material success, *eudaimonia* in Stoicism is achieved through the steadfast pursuit of virtue. Marcus Aurelius emphasizes this point in his *Meditations*: "When thou hast assumed these names, good, modest, true, rational, a man of equanimity, and magnanimous, take care that thou dost not change these names; and if thou shouldst lose them, quickly return to them." By cultivating a virtuous character, an individual ensures that their thoughts and actions are always aligned with the highest good, thus achieving true fulfillment.

PERSONAL INTEGRITY

The Stoics understood that by developing personal virtue and character, making difficult decisions becomes much easier. By fortifying one's moral character, a person does not even entertain decisions that are counter to their own moral code. When questionable, unethical, or illegal choices present themselves, a Stoic dismisses those options, choosing instead to maintain their integrity over possible gain or success from choices that would compromise their character. As Epictetus points out, "Ask me what the real good in man's case is, and I can only say that it is the right kind of moral character." For example, Cato the Younger, considered a man of impeccable character and virtue, chose death over supporting the tyrannical rule of Julius Caesar.

IMPACT ON THE LARGER WORLD

The Stoic commitment to virtue is not just self-serving. While the cultivation of personal virtue certainly aims at individual happiness, it also has a profound social dimension. Stoics believed that everyone is a part of the larger whole (humanity) and that their actions invariably affect this collective. When a person makes virtuous choices, it benefits the individual through strengthening their character, and it also benefits society. In short, cultivating virtue is your civic duty.

Seneca wrote extensively about the duty of the individual to contribute to the common good, emphasizing that "man is a social animal." This is where the virtue of justice becomes significant, guiding people to consider their welfare and the welfare of others in their actions. By practicing justice, a Stoic contributes to the harmony and functioning of society.

LIVING VIRTUOUSLY IN MODERN TIMES

The Stoic perspective on virtue is exceedingly relevant right now. Today, success is often measured by external achievements, but Stoicism asks people to return to the basics of character and integrity. This philosophy encourages you to reflect on your impact on others and the environment, promoting a life of responsibility and respect for the community.

The cultivation of virtue also allows you to navigate modern-day issues with grace and resilience. In dealing with personal challenges or societal injustices, a virtuous character gives you the strength to make good choices and maintain your composure.

The strengthening of one's character through the Stoic cultivation of virtue profoundly impacts not only one's personal life but also the world at large. By striving for *eudaimonia* through the practice of virtue, you realize your individual and community-oriented potential. Stoicism, therefore, offers a timeless reminder that the true measure of your life is the character you cultivate and the impact you have on the world around you.

IMPRESSIONS AND ASSENT

Testing Your Perceptions

Quotable Voices

"You can process in your intellect and senses a wealth
of thoughts and impressions simultaneously. There are
impressions that you assent to, others that you reject;
sometimes you suspend judgment altogether."

—Epictetus

Within Stoic philosophy, the concepts of impression and assent are
key to self-mastery and making rational choices. Stoics proposed
that if a person can correctly identify what they have perceived
externally, they're more likely to make better judgments. The Stoics
felt that one must clearly manage one's impressions because one's
senses and perceptions are what allow one to interact with the world.

Philosophical Definition

impressions: The Stoics defined impressions (*phantasia*) as the initial information or perceptions that come to a person from external stimuli. These are
things that one perceives through their physical senses, meaning anything that
a person can see, hear, touch, taste, or smell.

UNDERSTANDING IMPRESSIONS

The Stoics taught that impressions are involuntary; therefore, impressions are neutral until they are processed by reason. Stoics believed

this separation was important so that a person could rationally and objectively consider their perception before they ultimately judge what was perceived. Epictetus asks people to take their time and examine their impressions, saying, "Don't let the force of an impression when it first hit you knock you off your feet; just say to it: Hold on a moment; let me see who you are and what you represent. Let me put you to the test."

Philosophical Definition

assent: The Stoics defined assent (*sunkatathesis*) as the voluntary acceptance or agreement to an impression, which is crucial for forming beliefs and judgments. This is the space in between perceiving an impression and making a judgment.

THE ROLE OF ASSENT IN STOICISM

The Stoics believed that assent is the pivotal step in managing one's emotions because it is the moment where a person decides whether to let an impression turn into a judgment and a response. This space is where it is crucial to apply rationality and reason, rather than simply reacting to the initial impression.

EMOTIONAL REGULATION RELATING TO IMPRESSIONS AND ASSENT

By withholding assent from false or harmful impressions, a Stoic maintains their equanimity. Far too often, people believe something based on a first impression, without examining whether the impression is correct. In doing so, they make a quick judgment and react emotionally, often to their own detriment. The Stoics felt that by interrogating impressions, a person is more likely to dismiss incorrect ones, reducing errors in judgment and maintaining control over their emotions.

EXAMPLES OF IMPRESSIONS AND ASSENT

There are many examples of impressions and assent, such as the following.

Visual Illusions and Misperceptions

The Stoics felt that taking the time to interrogate one's impressions is crucial, because often perceptions are incorrect. Instances that easily illustrate how your perceptions can be fooled are illusions. For example, you might see a rope and mistake it for a snake or be tricked by the sleight-of-hand tricks of a street magician. In the art world, M.C. Escher combined different angles of perspectives to create scenes that can't exist in real life, such as never-ending staircases and infinite waterfalls.

Being Offended

Another example of where the Stoic practice of assent helps someone maintain their equilibrium is when they feel offended by another person. When another person speaks, it is your mind that interprets what was spoken, giving meaning to their words. It is possible that you misheard or misunderstood what was meant. Even if the person meant to provoke you, by practicing the Stoic concept of assent, you can pause to choose if and how you want to respond. "Remember, it is not enough to be hit or insulted to be harmed, you must believe that you are being harmed," Epictetus cautions. "If someone succeeds in provoking you, realize that your mind is complicit in the provocation. [...] Take a moment before reacting, and you will find it is easier to maintain control."

PRACTICAL EXERCISES FOR MANAGING IMPRESSIONS AND ASSENT

The following are some real-world exercises you can use to control your impressions and assent.

Pause and Reflect

From the moment you wake up, your senses are bombarded with information. Much of this is simply taken in and doesn't require a response. When you perceive an impression, taking a moment to consider what you have perceived and any judgments that you make about your perception is a simple and useful practice to strengthen your ability to assent to your impressions.

No Opinion

The Stoics taught that often people spend time focusing on things that they have no control over or have no impact on their lives. For example, celebrity gossip has no impact on a person's life, but it can take a lot of their time and energy. "You always own the option of having no opinion. There is never any need to get worked up or to trouble your soul about things you can't control. These things are not asking to be judged by you. Leave them alone," penned Marcus Aurelius. In this passage, Aurelius is saying that he can choose not to have an opinion on something, helping maintain his inner sense of calm.

By examining your perceptions, you exercise more control over your judgments and reactions. The Stoic practice of managing assent of your impressions is a powerful tool to improve your emotional well-being. As Seneca writes, "It's all in your head. You have the power to make things seem hard or easy or even amusing. The choice is yours."

THE ROLE OF PERSPECTIVE IN STOICISM

How Your Perspective Shapes Your Judgments
and Opinions

Quotable Voices

"If you are pained by any external thing, it is not this thing that
disturbs you, but your own judgment about it. And it is in your
power to wipe out this judgment now."

—Marcus Aurelius

Stoicism emphasizes the importance of perspective in shaping one's responses to the world. Your happiness and tranquility are determined not by external events but by the attitudes and interpretations you choose to adopt. Stoics believed that by managing one's perspectives, or attitude, toward external circumstances and events, one may be better able to weather the challenges of life calmly.

STOIC FOUNDATIONS ON PERSPECTIVE

At the heart of Stoicism lies the belief that only a person's judgments, responses, and perspectives are within their own direct control. External circumstances, while they can present challenges, do not inherently have the power to disturb one's peace unless allowed to. This core principle is vividly illustrated in the teachings of Epictetus, which support that it's your perspective—your interpretation—of events, rather than the events themselves, that governs your emotional and mental state.

DIFFERENCES BETWEEN PERCEPTIONS AND PERSPECTIVES

The Stoics made a clear distinction between perception and perspective. Your perceptions, the input that you receive through your senses, is something that is not under your power, whereas your perspective (attitude) toward the things that you perceive is under your control. Because you have power over your perspective, you have a choice in how you let the things you perceive affect you. Epictetus aptly observes this when he explains that people aren't afraid of the thing itself but by their ideas behind the thing. For more on the Stoic perspective on perception, see the Impressions and Assent section.

THE INFLUENCE OF PERSPECTIVE ON JUDGMENT

The reason why understanding and being aware of your perspectives is so important is because your perspective on something influences the judgments you make about it. Your biases and preconceptions can lead you to make incorrect judgments about what is really happening, leading you to make poor choices. Understanding your perspectives helps you to make more rational and reasonable judgments, leading to better outcomes.

A good example of how perspectives can influence your judgments is when it comes to dealing with other people. For example, if you have a negative attitude toward a coworker, then you may view every action or everything that person says negatively (even if their intentions are positive). Your perspective becomes the lens through which you filter every action they take. Being more objective in your attitude toward this person allows you to take things less personally, not assume the worst about them, and have a more productive work relationship.

HISTORICAL EXAMPLES AND STORIES

Stoic perspective has many historical examples, including the following.

Zeno and the Shipwreck

Zeno, the founder of Stoic philosophy, used his experiences to illustrate Stoic principles. After surviving a shipwreck and loss of material fortune, he reflected on how the event led to his philosophy studies. He reportedly said, "I made a prosperous voyage when I suffered [a] shipwreck." His perspective on the incident highlights how adopting a constructive viewpoint can transform adversity into personal growth.

Epictetus and the Lamp

There is a well-known anecdote where Epictetus had a lamp stolen from his household. When he replaced it with a cheaper one and that, too, was stolen, he remarked that it was only expected because the thief had gained from his previous theft. Epictetus used this incident to illustrate the Stoic lesson that a person's attachment to external things should be moderated by the perspective that they are impermanent and ultimately indifferent to their happiness.

Marcus Aurelius and the Art of Perspective

Even as a Roman emperor, Marcus Aurelius faced numerous challenges and personal struggles. He often reminded himself to be aware of his perspective to develop a more positive mindset. In reflecting on his perspectives, he writes, "[Instead of saying] 'I am unhappy, because this has happened to me.' Not so: say, 'I am happy, though this has happened to me, because I continue free from pain, neither crushed by the present nor fearing the future.'"

MODERN APPLICATIONS

The Stoic emphasis on perspective is not only historically significant but also exceedingly relevant in contemporary contexts. In modern psychological practices, such as cognitive behavioral therapy (CBT), the influence of perspective on emotional and mental health is widely recognized and utilized. CBT, much like Stoicism, teaches that changing a person's perspective on life's challenges can significantly alter emotional outcomes and lead to effective coping strategies.

Perspective in Stoicism is more than a passive lens through which a person views the world; it is an active tool that they can shape and utilize to maintain their tranquility and live virtuously. By choosing perspectives that align with reason and virtue, a Stoic aims to lead a resilient, fulfilling, and meaningful life. Through the wisdom of Stoic teachings, you see that the power to shape your life lies not in altering your external circumstances but in transforming your internal perspectives. As Marcus Aurelius notes, "Consider that everything is opinion, and opinion is in your power."

THE STOIC "VIEW FROM ABOVE"

Gaining Perspective and Tranquility

Quotable Voices

"We must take a higher view of all things,
and bear with them more easily: it better becomes a
man to scoff at life than to lament over it."

—Seneca

The "view from above" is a powerful Stoic exercise designed to enhance perspective and foster a sense of interconnectedness with the cosmos. This Stoic practice involves visualizing oneself from a high vantage point and looking down upon the inhabitants of the Earth and their activities. By adopting this broader perspective, you can transcend petty concerns, appreciate the transient nature of life, and cultivate a deeper sense of tranquility.

ORIGINS AND PHILOSOPHICAL UNDERPINNINGS

The "view from above" technique is deeply rooted in Stoic philosophy, which emphasizes the importance of perspective in achieving a life of virtue and peace. The Stoics believed that many of life's disturbances stem from a narrow viewpoint, overly focused on the self and its immediate concerns.

Marcus Aurelius often practiced the "view from above" technique to remind himself of his place in the universe: "Look at the past—empire succeeding empire—and from that, extrapolate the future: the same thing. No escape from the rhythm of events. Which is why observing life for forty years is as good as a thousand. Would you really see anything new?"

RELATION TO *MEMENTO MORI*

The "view from above" is like the Stoic practice of *Memento Mori*. *Memento Mori*, Latin for "remember that you must die," is about keeping perspective of oneself in the measure of time. The "view from above" is about picturing oneself along the measure of space. Each of these exercises may help you develop a perspective of your place in the cosmos and focus on what matters. To learn more about *Memento Mori*, see the section on *Memento Mori*.

PRACTICAL APPLICATIONS OF THE "VIEW FROM ABOVE"

The "view from above" has many applicable day-to-day situations, like the following.

Reduction of Ego

By visualizing yourself from a great height, you appear small and as one among many. When you adopt this perspective, it helps reduce your ego and its demands because you see the minor role of your personal problems in the grand scheme of things.

Enhanced Empathy

When you take the time to see the interconnectedness of all humans from this elevated view, it fosters a sense of empathy and connection. Recognizing that others face similar challenges and joys can deepen your empathy and compassion.

Cultivation of Tranquility

The "view from above" puts daily struggles into perspective, reminding you that many of your worries are trivial when viewed against the backdrop of the cosmos. When you recognize that your daily worries about trivial gossip at a party will not be remembered in fifty years, that realization can lead to profound inner peace.

Mindfulness

Like other mindfulness practices, the Stoic "view from above" can be a form of meditation that helps you detach from your immediate surroundings and emotions, leading to greater calm and less reactivity.

Coping with Stress

In stressful situations, imagining your problems from a cosmic perspective can provide immediate relief and a reevaluation of what is truly important, helping to focus on solutions rather than problems. By seeing your problems from a distance, it can give you a clearer perspective on the importance, or lack thereof, of the annoyances and frustrations of daily life.

The Stoic "view from above" is a timeless tool that offers a unique way of looking at life's challenges. It's a practical model on changing your perspective to change your emotional responses. By regularly practicing this visualization, you can cultivate a greater appreciation for your place in the cosmos, reduce your everyday anxieties, and approach life with a renewed sense of purpose and tranquility. Adopting a more expansive perspective can remind you that your concerns, while significant to you, are but small ripples in the vast ocean of existence.

EXAMPLES OF THE "VIEW FROM ABOVE"

Marcus Aurelius provides a vivid example of this practice in his *Meditations*:

"You can rid yourself of many useless things among those that disturb you, for they lie entirely in your imagination; and you will then gain for yourself ample space by comprehending the whole universe in your mind, and by contemplating the eternity of time, and observing the rapid change of every part of everything, how short is the time from birth to dissolution, and the illimitable time before birth as well as the equally boundless time after dissolution."

—Marcus Aurelius

When you contemplate the length of time from the beginning of the universe to your birth, and the infinite amount of time after your death, you can see how insignificantly short your life is.

Astronomy and Perspective

Modern astronomy offers a literal "view from above" with its images of Earth from space. Astronauts often speak of the profound impact of seeing our planet as a small, fragile blue dot in the vastness of space. Astronomer Carl Sagan gave a modern take on the "view from above," writing about a picture of the Earth taken from the *Voyager* spacecraft: "Look again at that dot. That's here. That's home. That's us. On it everyone you love, everyone you know, everyone you ever heard of, every human being who ever was, lived out their lives."

The Continuous Play of Humanity

Seneca likens life to an ongoing play of humanity, urging people to play their parts well: "There's no difference between the one and the other—you didn't exist and you won't exist—you've got no concern with either period. As it is with a play, so it is with life—what matters is not how long the acting lasts, but how good it is. It is not important at what point you stop. Stop wherever you will—only make sure that you round it off with a good ending."

FREEDOM FROM EXTERNAL EVENTS

Embracing the Power Within

Quotable Voices

"Look within, for within is the wellspring of virtue, which will not cease flowing, if you cease not from digging."

—Marcus Aurelius

In the pursuit of tranquility and virtue, Stoic philosophy offers a powerful framework: freedom from external events. Stoicism teaches that true peace comes not from controlling the external world but from mastering one's reactions to it. Stoicism empowers individuals to achieve freedom from external events by cultivating inner strength and resilience.

STOIC PRINCIPLES OF INNER FREEDOM

A core principle of Stoic philosophy is the distinction between what is within one's control and what is not. The Stoics asserted that a person's thoughts, beliefs, and reactions are within their own power, while external events—ranging from the weather to the actions of others—are beyond their direct control. Epictetus, one of the key Stoic thinkers, succinctly encapsulates this in his *Enchiridion*: "Some things are in our control and others not." By focusing on the former and detaching from the latter, Stoics maintain equanimity in the face of life's unpredictability.

MASTERING RESPONSES TO EXTERNAL EVENTS

Stoicism teaches that freedom comes from the mastery of one's responses to external events. This mastery involves reshaping one's perceptions and judgments, which are often the real sources of one's distress. Roman emperor-philosopher Marcus Aurelius advises in his *Meditations*: "If you are distressed by anything external, the pain is not due to the thing itself, but to your estimate of it; and this you have the power to revoke at any moment." By changing your internal responses, you not only ease your suffering; you also reclaim your freedom.

THE DICHOTOMY OF CONTROL

A key concept in Stoicism is the Dichotomy of Control, which advises a person to accept whatever they cannot change while striving to influence what they can. This principle is a practical approach to living; it encourages focusing on personal effort and ethics rather than the outcomes, which are often unpredictable and influenced by external factors. This mindset not only reduces anxiety and frustration; it also fosters a sense of serenity and empowerment. As Epictetus succinctly explains, "Suffering arises from trying to control what is uncontrollable, or from neglecting what is within our power." For more on this topic, see The Dichotomy of Control section.

The Stoics understood that most of a person's negative emotions occur because of their perspective on external, uncontrollable events. Whether your emotions are in response to, for example, others' opinions of you, a stock market loss, or a natural disaster, the

Stoics recognized that getting angry or stressed over situations outside of your control often leads to poor choices and can often make the situation worse. As Marcus Aurelius observes, "How much more grievous are the consequences of anger than the causes of it."

AMOR FATI

The Stoic concept of *Amor Fati*, to "love one's fate," is central to the Stoic idea of freedom from external events. Rather than reluctantly accepting what happens in life, the Stoics proposed that people should learn to love and appreciate all the challenges that life sends their way. They believed that rather than wasting time and energy and disturbing one's inner calm by resisting the events of life, it's better to cultivate a perspective that everything external in life is an opportunity to practice virtue.

HISTORICAL EXAMPLES OF STOIC FREEDOM

Stoic freedom can be seen throughout history in many ways, like the following.

Cato the Younger

Known for his unwavering Stoic virtue, Cato the Younger exhibited remarkable resilience and independence in the face of political turmoil during the final days of the Roman Republic. His commitment to Stoic principles allowed him to maintain his integrity and freedom even as external events spiraled beyond his control.

James Stockdale

An American vice admiral and aviator, Stockdale was a prisoner of war for over seven years during the Vietnam War. He credits Stoic philosophy, particularly the teachings of Epictetus, with giving him the inner strength to endure captivity and torture without breaking. His survival and leadership under such extreme conditions demonstrate how Stoic wisdom can provide profound resilience.

MODERN APPLICATION
OF STOIC FREEDOM

In today's fast-paced and often volatile world, the Stoic practice of distinguishing between the controllable and uncontrollable aspects of life is more relevant than ever. For individuals facing challenges at work, in personal relationships, or in broader societal issues, Stoicism offers a way to navigate stress and adversity with grace. By focusing on your internal reactions and maintaining your ethical standards, you can achieve a form of freedom that external circumstances cannot diminish.

The Stoic path to freedom from external events is not about indifference but about active engagement with the world without being dominated by it. It involves a deep transformation of your perspective, where peace is derived not from external conditions but from a well-fortified inner life. As Epictetus puts it, "We, not externals, are the masters of our judgments." In embracing Stoic freedom, you find not only freedom but also the resilience to live your life with purpose and dignity, no matter what challenges you face.

EUDAIMONIA

The Stoic Conception of Happiness

Quotable Voices

"The happy life is a life that is in harmony with its own nature."

—Seneca

In Stoic philosophy, *eudaimonia* is achieved by living in accordance with nature and reason, which involves understanding and aligning with the *Logos* (the rational structure of the universe) and living a life of virtue. The Stoics believed that virtue is both necessary and sufficient for *eudaimonia,* meaning that living virtuously is all a person needs to have a truly good and fulfilling life.

Philosophical Definition

eudaimonia: A Greek term often translated as "happiness," "welfare," or more accurately, "flourishing" or "living well." It is a concept widely used in ancient Greek philosophy, not just by the Stoics but also by Aristotle, Socrates, and other philosophers. *Eudaimonia* represents the ultimate goal of human life, the highest good that is achieved through the practice of virtue.

HISTORICAL CONTEXT OF *EUDAIMONIA*

The concept of *eudaimonia* was present throughout many of the Socratic philosophers; it was a departure from the pre-Socratic philosophers. *Eudaimonia* was later redefined by the Stoics to align with their ideas of living in accordance with human nature, as well as the nature of the world and the cosmos.

Democritus

While the pre-Socratic philosophers were mainly concerned with understanding the nature of the world and the underlying principles governing change and stability in the universe, Democritus delved into ethical questions more than his predecessors. Democritus is considered a bridge between the pre-Socratic and Socratic philosophers, proposing ideas about happiness and "the good life" that are echoed in later ethical theories. He believed in living a cheerful life (euthymia) where one's contentment comes from an inner state of mind rather than external circumstances.

Socrates

Socrates moved the conversation in philosophy from trying to understand the underpinnings of the universe to understanding what made a happy, fulfilling life. For Socrates, *eudaimonia* was the goal of human life and could be achieved through the pursuit of wisdom and virtue. Socrates considered virtue to be a kind of wisdom one attained by understanding what is truly good. He believed people only do evil from a lack of knowledge, reflecting: "The bad one is that way because of the ignorance, therefore he can be healed with wisdom."

Plato

Plato expanded the Socratic idea of *eudaimonia* in his dialogues, most notably in *The Republic*. He felt that *eudaimonia* was the result of a well-ordered soul that was governed by reason and in harmony with itself. Creating this type of soul eventually led to a just and happy life. Plato also felt that self-sufficiency was a key to happiness, writing, "The man who makes everything that leads to happiness depend upon himself, and not upon other men, has adopted the very best plan for living happily."

Aristotle

Aristotle took a more systematic approach to cultivating *eudaimonia* in a person's life in his *Nicomachean Ethics*, where he describes it as the highest good and the ultimate aim of all human actions. He writes, "Happiness is the meaning and the purpose of life, the whole aim and end of human existence." He proposed the idea that happiness could be found in the "Golden Mean," meaning that virtue is found in a balance between excess and deficiency.

Epicurus

A contemporary of Zeno of Citium and founder of Epicureanism, Epicurus had a different take on *eudaimonia*. He identified pleasure as the highest good but distinguished between types of pleasures. Epicurus emphasized simple pleasures, the absence of pain (aponia), and freedom from disturbance (ataraxia) as the path to happiness. For Epicureans, the wise pursuit of pleasure, moderated by knowledge and temperance, leads to *eudaimonia*.

STOIC *EUDAIMONIA*

The Stoics believed that *eudaimonia* was achieved by the rational control of one's emotions and desires (a concept called *apatheia*) and living a life of virtue and reason. They also proposed that one must live according to the rational nature of the universe (*Logos*) by embracing whatever happens as necessary and just.

The Stoics also felt that a person only needed to live a life of virtue, namely the virtues of wisdom, courage, justice, and temperance, in order to achieve happiness. This was a departure from Aristotle's view that fame, fortune, and beauty were also necessary for human flourishing. Seneca clarifies this, writing, "A good character is the only guarantee of everlasting, carefree happiness."

UTILITARIANISM

The idea of *eudaimonia* is not just limited to ancient philosophy. In the more contemporary philosophy of Utilitarianism, John Stuart Mill, a nineteenth-century British philosopher and economist, proposed that all activity (including economic and political) should be aimed at helping people achieve happiness. He writes, "The utilitarian doctrine is, that happiness is desirable, and the only thing desirable, as an end; all other things being only desirable as means to that end."

Overall, the concept of *eudaimonia* has been a key component of philosophy since the days of Socrates. It marked a shift in philosophy from the pursuit of understanding the makeup of the universe to exploring what it takes to live a happy and flourishing life. The Stoics, with their pursuit of reducing things to their simplest and most effective form, proposed that one only needed virtue, *apatheia*, and alignment with the *Logos* in order to achieve *eudaimonia*.

STOICISM ON WEALTH, FAME, AND EXTERNAL GOODS

Cultivating Virtue in the Face of "Indifferents"

Quotable Voices

"The essence of good and evil consists in the condition of our character. And externals are the means by which our character finds its particular good and evil."

—Epictetus

The Stoics believed that a person only needed to live a virtuous life to be happy. They argued that Externals (anything not under one's control) were "indifferent," meaning that they were neither good nor bad but things with which to develop one's virtue against. Living a virtuous life, you should be able to find inner peace and contentment in any situation.

Philosophical Definition

"indifferent": Something that is neither good nor bad but can be used in a positive or negative way. As an example, a knife is neutral until it is used to either cook a meal (positive) or hurt another person (negative). In Stoicism, external things, events, and circumstances are neutral and only become good or bad based on how a person responds to or uses them.

THE STOIC PERSPECTIVE ON WEALTH

The Stoic philosophers came from all walks of life. Stoicism's founder, Zeno of Citium, was a wealthy merchant, but he lived a spare, ascetic lifestyle. Epictetus was born enslaved and walked with a limp after being beaten by his master. Seneca was a wealthy merchant and councilor to Nero. Marcus Aurelius was the emperor of Rome, arguably the richest and most powerful man in the world at the time. Each of them understood that wealth and power weren't the sources of true happiness but that happiness came from self-mastery and virtue.

The Stoics held that wealth should be used wisely and justly, in accordance with virtue. Wealth was considered neither good nor bad but "indifferent," and should be used to develop virtue. The Stoics understood how wealth, if not used properly, could damage one's character and cause suffering just as much as being poor.

"Wealth is the slave of a wise man. The master of a fool," writes Seneca, suggesting that if a person is not careful, wealth can rule over them, and that the pursuit of wealth can cause discontentment and suffering, leaving one dissatisfied and always wanting more.

Epictetus went even further, with the reminder that acquiring wealth was not in one's power, but acquiring happiness is: "Examine yourself whether you wish to be rich or to be happy. If you wish to be rich, you should know that it is neither a good thing nor at all in your power: but if you wish to be happy, you should know that it is both a good thing and in your power, for the one is a temporary loan of fortune, and happiness comes from the will."

External Goods

For the Stoics, material goods were things that should be enjoyed in moderation; a person should avoid extravagances and excess that often come in the pursuit of wealth. Epictetus recognized the unhappiness that can come with seeking wealth, stating, "Wealth consists not in having great possessions, but in having few wants." By controlling your desires and reducing your material wants, you can be content with what you have and find inner peace.

The Stoics also taught that one should not have emotional attachments to material possessions, as they are lost as easily as they are acquired. Epictetus proposes, "Under no circumstances ever say 'I have lost something,' only 'I returned it.'" By not being too attached to material possessions, you can maintain your equanimity when those things are lost or broken.

Power

"All cruelty springs from weakness," writes Seneca, noting that the abuse of power stems from a weakness of character. The Stoics understood that power could just as easily be used for good as for evil. Therefore, it was paramount for a person to develop virtue to avoid the excesses that befall those with power. They believed that those with power had a responsibility to use that power for good rather than personal enrichment.

The Proper Use of Wealth and Power

Marcus Aurelius used the power and wealth of the Roman Empire, as well as his own personal wealth, for the betterment of those he governed. He invested in welfare programs to educate, feed, and train orphans and needy children, and other programs to help rehabilitate soldiers involved in the many conflicts under his reign. During the plague that ravaged Rome, he even sold many of his personal possessions to help raise funds for the relief of the victims. For Aurelius, wealth was a means to help those less fortunate, to alleviate the suffering of others, and to cultivate the virtue of justice over an indulgence in personal luxury.

FAME AND REPUTATION

Since the thoughts and actions of others are outside of one's control, Stoicism teaches that a person's reputation is not theirs to change. The Stoics felt that one should act in accordance with virtue, regardless of what others might think. Epictetus states, "If you wish to be well spoken of, learn to speak well (of others): and when you have learned to speak well of them, try to act well, and so you will reap the fruit of being well spoken of."

Stoicism teaches that it's one's conduct and character that one should focus on, not the opinions of others. Seneca writes, "No one, I think, rates virtue higher or is more consecrated to virtue than he who has lost his reputation for being a good man in order to keep from losing the approval of his conscience." He understood that, by focusing on virtue, a person is more likely to act well than be tempted to do things for the approval of others.

The idea that material possessions, wealth, and fame can bring happiness is not a new idea but rather something that has been a part of the human condition since recorded history. However, the Stoics taught that true happiness comes from your internal state. As Marcus Aurelius sums up, "Very little is needed to make a happy life; it is all within yourself, in your way of thinking."

ACHIEVING *EUDAIMONIA*

Practical Steps to Happiness

The Stoics had a clear idea of how to achieve *eudaimonia*: practicing rational control over one's emotions, living a life of virtue, understanding what one has control over, and accepting events outside of one's influence.

But as with most things, this is easier said than done. How can you live a virtuous life? How do you apply rationality over your emotions? What if the circumstances and events that happen in your life feel overwhelming? Fortunately, the Stoics had high ideals about what it takes to live a good life, but they also provided tools to help in that pursuit.

FOCUS ON WHAT YOU CAN CONTROL

The Stoics believed a key part of achieving *eudaimonia* is to understand what one does and does not have control over. By focusing on the things you can control, you can actually make progress. When you fail to act on the things under your control, you become a victim of external circumstances and events. By focusing on your responses, you are better able to navigate the ups and downs of life.

LET GO OF WHAT YOU
CANNOT CONTROL

"Circumstances do not rise to meet our expectations. Events happen as they do. People behave as they are. Embrace what you actually get," says Epictetus, suggesting that by aligning one's desires with reality, a person is able to deal with the real world. If something is outside your control, regardless of the effort you put in, you will not make any progress. Instead, you'll cause yourself unnecessary suffering and frustration.

MANAGING EMOTIONS

Stoics placed immense importance on controlling one's emotions. When something upsets you, you should use your rationality to decide how you want to respond, rather than simply reacting. Marcus Aurelius states, "If you are pained by any external thing, it is not this thing that disturbs you, but your own judgment about it. And it is in your power to wipe out this judgment now."

For example, if someone cuts you off in traffic, your first reaction might be anger, believing that the other driver purposefully cut you off. Rather than seeking retaliation, the Stoic response would be to back off and let the other driver go on their way. By thinking rationally, you can decide that safety is more important than satiating your desire for revenge. While you cannot control the other person's actions, you can control your focus on driving safely.

CULTIVATING CONTENTMENT

Seneca provided a clear outline of how to reduce anxiety and find contentment in everyday life. In his *Moral Letters to Lucilius*, Seneca writes, "True happiness is to enjoy the present, without anxious dependence upon the future, not to amuse ourselves with either hopes or fears but to rest satisfied with what we have, which is sufficient, for he that is so wants nothing." By learning to be content with what you have in life and not worrying about what the future may or may not bring, you can find happiness in the present moment.

LIVING WITH VIRTUE

In Stoicism, living with virtue is paramount to achieving *eudaimonia*. Virtue focuses on how you live, not a prescription of what you do. "We must take care to live not merely a long life, but a full one," Seneca explains. "For living a long life requires only good fortune, but living a full life requires character. Long is the life that is fully lived; it is fulfilled only when the mind supplies its own good qualities and empowers itself from within."

When you live with virtue, then your choices and actions are filtered through the lens of your principles. Before taking any action, you should examine it to make sure that it aligns with your values. Ask yourself, "Is this wise and just? Am I acting with courage? Am I acting with moderation or giving into excess?" If you live a virtuous life, rather than simply following your desires, you lead a life of balance and integrity.

COMMUNITY AND RELATIONSHIPS

Marcus Aurelius writes, "Injustice is impiety. For since the universal nature has made rational animals for the sake of one another to help one another according to their desserts, but in no way to injure one another, he who transgresses her will is clearly guilty of impiety toward the highest divinity." Since the Stoics believed that humans are social animals, the importance of acting justly in the treatment of others helps to create social harmony, moving humankind closer to *eudaimonia*. By treating others with compassion and practicing the four virtues in your personal relationships and in public life, you strengthen social bonds and improve society.

EMBRACING CHALLENGES

Obstacles, according to the Stoics, are opportunities for growth and cultivation of virtue. Rather than roadblocks, challenges are how you develop virtue. Handling situations in life justly, with courage, wisdom, and self-discipline, is how you live a good life. You cannot simply study virtue but must put virtue into action.

Eudaimonia is not a place you reach but a state of mind and way of achieving inner peace while dealing with everyday challenges. With that end in mind, your choices and actions align with the goal of human flourishing, not just for yourself but for society as a whole.

THE *LOGOS*

The Stoic Worldview and Cosmic Nature

Quotable Voices

"All things are implicated with one another, and the bond is holy; and there is hardly anything unconnected with any other thing. For things have been coordinated, and they combine to form the same universe."

—Marcus Aurelius

The Stoics believed that the universe is not a random assembly of atoms but is organized and maintained by a rational structure called the *Logos*. This rationality is purposeful, aiming toward order and goodness. For the Stoics, because the universe is rational, all events are part of a larger, beneficial design, even those things that appear detrimental or chaotic in the short term.

Philosophical Definition

Logos: The concept of the *Logos* is central to Stoic philosophy, encompassing a broad and profound belief of the universe's rational structure. Originating from the Greek word meaning "word," "principle," or "reason," the Stoic *Logos* is the rational principle that governs the cosmos. This concept is deeply intertwined with Stoic physics, ethics, and logic, and it is a foundational principle that explains the nature of the universe and human behavior.

THE *LOGOS* AS COSMIC RATIONALITY

In Stoic philosophy, the *Logos* is considered the divine, animating principle of the universe, which orders and defines the structure and function of all things. Overall, the *Logos* ensures that the universe operates in a rational and purposeful manner. This worldview posits that everything happens for a reason, and that reason is aligned with the rational, logical structure of the cosmos. Marcus Aurelius notes this in *Meditations*, writing, "Everything that happens, happens as it should, and if you observe carefully, you will find this to be so."

THE *LOGOS* AND NATURE

The Stoics argued that because human beings possess reason, they are part of the rational order of the *Logos*. This shared rationality underpins the Stoic concept to live "according to nature." So, a person should live in alignment with the rationality that structures both nature and human nature. By understanding and adhering to the rational structure of the *Logos*, humans fulfill their true nature and achieve *eudaimonia*.

THE *LOGOS* IN INDIVIDUAL LIVES

The Stoic concept of the *Logos* holds that everyone has the capacity to use reason to control their responses to external events. Human emotions and desires are not inherently bad but become problematic when they're based on incorrect judgments or when they disrupt living in harmony with the *Logos*. You should therefore cultivate a rational mind that sees the world clearly, understands the nature of good and evil, and responds appropriately to life's challenges.

The Stoics also believed in an ethical dimension of the *Logos*, which frames virtue as living in harmony with reason. For the Stoics, the cardinal virtues of wisdom, justice, courage, and temperance are necessary to living in accordance with the *Logos*. By practicing Stoic virtues, you can align your thoughts and actions with the rational, orderly way the cosmos works.

DETERMINISM AND THE *LOGOS*

The Stoic concept of the *Logos* incorporates elements of both determinism and free will. They believed that the *Logos* is deterministic in nature, and that everything in the universe happens according to a purposeful cosmic plan (described as fate or providence). Stoics felt this determinism was not merely physical but also moral and rational, and that the universe was not only ordered but also just. Chrysippus, a Stoic of few remaining texts, writes, "If something were brought about without an antecedent cause, it would be untrue that all things come about through fate. But if it is plausible that all events have an antecedent cause, what ground can be offered for not conceding that all things come about through fate?" Here he explains that everything that happens is caused by something that happened before it, and he therefore concludes that everything is determined by fate.

FREE WILL AND THE *LOGOS*

Despite their deterministic view of the universe, the Stoics also believed in the importance of individual agency. They held that humans, through their capacity for reason, can align themselves with the rational order of the *Logos*. The Stoics thought that while a person cannot control the events that happen to them, they have the power to control their reactions to the events and make ethical, rational choices.

RECONCILING DETERMINISM AND FREE WILL

The Stoics resolved the tension between determinism and free will through the concept of "appropriate actions" (or *kathēkonta* in Greek). The Stoics believed that one should take actions in accordance with one's role and the nature of the universe. By understanding and aligning with the rational structure of the cosmos, you can use your rationality—your form of free will. Marcus Aurelius refers to this, writing, "The universe is change; our life is what our thoughts make it."

The Stoic *Logos* is a comprehensive principle of rationality that spans the cosmos, dictates the natural order, and guides human behavior. Living in accordance with the *Logos* means you understand and embrace your role within this vast, interconnected, rational universe by leading a life of virtue and rationality. By aligning yourself with the *Logos*, you can achieve true peace and contentment.

LIVING ACCORDING TO NATURE

Being a Rational and Social Animal

Quotable Voices

"To the rational animal the same act is at once
according to nature and according to reason."

—Marcus Aurelius

Living according to nature is a key component of the Stoic philosophy and involves aligning one's actions with the rational and social nature inherent to human beings. This means acting in a way that is consistent with reason and fulfilling your duties as a social creature who cares for others.

DEFINITION OF NATURE

The Stoics defined nature as the surrounding world, including the universe. Just as a tiger is a skilled hunter using its natural attributes of claws, teeth, and speed to capture its prey, humans should use their traits of rationality and social nature to be the best humans possible.

Rational Nature

Stoicism argues that reason is part of human nature, and therefore one should act rationally, rather than giving into one's animal instincts. "And so it is inexcusable for man to begin and end where the beasts do," teaches Epictetus. "He should begin where they do, but only end where nature left off dealing with him; which is to say, in contemplation and understanding." Ultimately, the Stoics acknowledged that humans have much in common with animals, but that through reasoning, they can rise above their animal instincts and live with virtue.

Social Nature

Stoicism emphasizes the interconnectedness of all things, arguing that individuals are part of a larger community. Living according to nature involves recognizing this interconnectedness and acting in ways that support the common good. As Marcus Aurelius notes, "Let this first be established: that I am a part of the whole that is governed by nature; next, that I stand in some intimate connection with other kindred parts."

Harmony with the Universe

Stoics believed that the universe is governed by a rational order, the *Logos*, and that living according to nature means accepting this order and living in harmony with it. This includes accepting one's fate and the events that occur, seeing them as part of a greater rational plan. However, Stoics also emphasized personal agency, advocating that people should act virtuously regardless of any predetermined outcomes.

Virtue As Nature

Virtue is the highest good in Stoicism. In fact, the Stoics said that humans, by living according to virtue, are living according to their nature. Musonius Rufus, who mentored Epictetus, proposes that virtue is a core part of all humans, writing, "The human being is born with an inclination toward virtue." Epictetus further elaborates on what happens when human beings act against their nature:

"A plant or animal fares poorly when it acts contrary to its nature; and a human being is no different. Well, then, biting, kicking, wanton imprisonment, and beheading—is that what our nature entails? No; rather, acts of kindness, cooperation, and goodwill. And so, whether you like it or not, a person fares poorly whenever he acts like an insensitive brute."

—Epictetus

Emotion As a Natural Response

While Stoicism is sometimes misinterpreted as emotionless, it actually recognizes emotions as natural responses. The Stoic approach is to understand and manage emotions through reason, rather than being ruled by them. Marcus Aurelius urges people to not let external circumstances control their responses and act against their nature. He asks, "Does what's happened keep you from acting with justice, generosity, self-control, sanity, prudence, honesty, humility, straightforwardness, and all other qualities that allow a person's nature to fulfill itself?"

Accepting Your Nature

For the Stoics, part of living according to nature means that a person accepts their role in life and work to live according to virtue within society. Epictetus says an individual must accept themselves for who they are and play their role to the best of their ability:

"Reflect on the other social roles you play. If you are a council member, consider what a council member should do. If you are young, what does being young mean, if you are old, what does age imply, if you are a father, what does fatherhood entail? Each of our titles, when reflected upon, suggests the acts appropriate to it."

—Epictetus

In short, the Stoics believed that a person should accept their traits, abilities, and station in life, and make the best of the circumstances they find themselves in. So, by not resisting what happens in life but rather working with what life brings your way, you are able to make the biggest impact in the world.

Accepting Others' Nature

"Where is the harm or the strangeness in the boor acting like a boor? See whether you are not yourself the more to blame in not expecting that he would err in such a way," writes Marcus Aurelius, reminding himself that others will act according to their nature, and one should deal with them as they are, not how one wishes them to be. As Epictetus further elaborates, "Is a brother unjust? Well, preserve your own just relation toward him. Consider not what he does, but what you are to do to keep your own will in a state conformable to nature, for another cannot hurt you unless you please. You will then be hurt when you consent to be hurt."

The Stoic concept of living according to nature involves a profound engagement with your inner rationality and external duties. This Stoic principle remains profoundly relevant even today, offering insights into how you might find harmony and purpose in a complex world.

APATHEIA

The Theory of Emotions in Stoicism

The Stoics felt that mastering one's emotions was key to achieving *eudaimonia*. The Stoic theory of emotions is called *apatheia*, which is achieved by mastering your reactions to desires, aversions, and the emotions stemming from misjudgments. The goal of *apatheia* is not to eliminate feelings but to prevent irrational and excessive emotions that disturb the mind.

Philosophical Definitions

passion: The Stoic use of *passion* comes from the Greek word *pathos*, a wide-ranging term meaning "an infliction one suffers." Passions included anger, fear, anguish, and excessive joy. Passions, in the Stoic sense, are any overwhelming emotions that override a person's ability for reason and rationality.

apatheia: A Greek word from the prefix *a-* meaning "without" and *pathos*, meaning "suffering" or "passion," *apatheia* implies freedom from the distress caused by unnecessary desires and irrational emotions. It's not the same as the modern English word *apathy*, meaning "indifference" or "impassiveness." Stoics strive for *apatheia*—to avoid being swayed by emotions like fear, anger, or excessive pleasure, which can cloud judgment and lead to irrational actions.

THE FOUNDATIONS OF *APATHEIA*

The Stoics believed in the *Logos*, a rational and deterministic structure that organizes the universe. They also believed that rational humans are meant to live in harmony with this order. By using one's reason and rationality, one can judge things correctly, and therefore, one's emotional response to events and circumstances is appropriate, keeping one free from suffering and maintaining inner peace.

In contrast, when a person resists this natural order and fails to use their rationality, they allow themself to be overcome with *pathos* (passions). In doing so, they suffer and cause suffering to others because of their reactions to events. In his essay *De Ira (On Anger)*, Seneca argues this succinctly: "Anger, if not restrained, is frequently more hurtful to us than the injury that provokes it."

RELATIONSHIP BETWEEN *APATHEIA* AND *EUDAIMONIA*

While *apatheia* and *eudaimonia* are distinct concepts, they are closely related within Stoic philosophy. *Apatheia* is seen as crucial for achieving *eudaimonia*. By maintaining a state of emotional equilibrium, you can make rational decisions based on virtue, living in accordance with nature and achieving the Stoic ideal of flourishing. The cultivation of *apatheia* helps people focus on what truly matters, which directly contributes to *eudaimonia*. *Eudaimonia* encompasses not only emotional stability (*apatheia*) but also the active practice of virtues in interactions with others and the world.

THOUGHTS AND EMOTIONS

Another key aspect of *apatheia* is understanding how one's thoughts and perspective cause one's emotional reactions to external events and circumstances. Since emotions are the drivers for a person's choices and actions, the Stoics insisted that one should be mindful of the influence their perspective has on their judgments. Seneca, on how the influence of perspective causes personal suffering, writes, "We are more often frightened than hurt; and we suffer more from imagination than from reality." Essentially, it's a person's thoughts that cause their emotions, so the more you can be aware of and manage your thoughts, the more control you have over your emotions.

CONTROL

The Stoics felt that understanding what one has control of plays a crucial role in *apatheia*. Seneca argues, "What is freedom, you ask? It means not being a slave to any circumstance, to any constraint, to any chance." When you can let go of things outside of your control and focus on what you have control over, then you free yourself of unnecessary stress, anxiety, and fear.

OBJECTIVITY

By providing a lens for understanding individual perspectives and biases, Stoicism helps people view things more objectively and use their rationality to judge things correctly. When you can view events without the bias of personal judgments, you can more clearly see things for what they are, and not let your emotions cloud your judgment. Marcus Aurelius illustrates this by saying, "Look beneath the surface; let not the several quality of a thing nor its worth escape thee." This passage suggests delving deeper into the essence of things, beyond superficial appearances, to grasp their true nature and value.

The Stoics also argued that people don't have to take things so seriously, and they can use humor to keep their objectivity balanced. For example, Epictetus once quipped, "If someone speaks badly of you, do not defend yourself against the accusations, but reply, 'You obviously don't know about my other vices, otherwise you would have mentioned these as well.'"

The principle of *apatheia* is a key part of Stoicism. Overall, Stoics argued that by correctly judging external events and circumstances over which one has little or no control, one should be able to react properly, and thereby find oneself in accordance with nature rather than resisting it. In short, if you can't control something, why get upset about it?

EMOTIONAL RESILIENCE AND ACCEPTANCE

Keep Calm and Carry On

Quotable Voices
"Be like the promontory against which the waves continually break; but it stands firm and tames the fury of the water around it."
—Marcus Aurelius

The Stoics understood the power that emotions have over the human mind. These emotions are the fuel that powers human behavior for better or worse. The Stoics advocated for the rational domestication of emotions, not that they should be eliminated. Stoicism teaches the acceptance of what one cannot control and focuses on harnessing one's reactions to external events.

UNDERSTANDING STOIC EMOTIONAL RESILIENCE

In order to understand Stoic emotional resilience, it's best to first contextualize it with other Stoic teachings.

The Dichotomy of Control

Stoic philosophy hinges on the Dichotomy of Control, which instructs that each individual needs to have a clear understanding of what is in their control and what is not. The Dichotomy of Control teaches that emotional resilience comes from focusing one's energy on what one can control—one's responses, beliefs, and actions. To learn more about the Dichotomy of Control, see its section earlier in this book.

Apatheia

The Stoic concept of *apatheia*, meaning "without passions," is a guide to developing emotional resilience. For Stoics, the term *passions* meant any negative emotions such as anger or fear, and they proposed controlling these negative emotions to keep one's sense of self-control. To learn more about *apatheia*, see the *Apatheia* section.

Objective Representation

By learning to use one's rationality, realizing what one has control over, and recognizing the influence of one's perspective on one's emotional state, the Stoics believed a person could better cultivate a sense of inner peace and contentment in almost any situation. By viewing events objectively and approaching situations with a calm and rational outlook, you can make decisions without being overrun by your emotions.

STOIC EMOTIONAL ACCEPTANCE

The Stoics prioritized emotional acceptance by using the following concepts as tools.

Indifference to "Indifferents"

Stoics taught about the concept of "indifferents," referring to external things that don't affect one's moral character (like wealth or health). They believed that while some "indifferents" are preferable, they should not disturb one's emotional equilibrium. Marcus Aurelius argues, "Things do not touch the soul, for they are external and remain immovable; so our perturbations come only from our inner opinions."

Sympatheia

The Stoics believed in the concept of *sympatheia*, or the interconnectivity of the universe, which proposes that everything happens as part of a larger reason. Marcus Aurelius encouraged viewing life's events as necessary and thus accepting them with tranquility: "Think of the universal substance, of which you have a very small portion; and of universal time, of which a short and indivisible interval has been assigned to you; and of that which is fixed by destiny, and how small a part of it you are."

Amor Fati

Friedrich Nietzsche, who greatly admired Stoic philosophy, termed the acceptance of one's fate as *Amor Fati*, or love of one's fate. In other words, by learning to love everything that happens, external events and circumstances don't influence your emotions as much. If there is something that you don't have control over, then getting upset or angry about it is pointless and unproductive. So, *Amor Fati* is the practical application of *sympatheia*. Epictetus advocated for a harmonious acceptance of circumstances, overall encouraging people to wish for the predetermined outcome, regardless of how the chips fall. To read more about *Amor Fati*, see its section later in this book.

EXAMPLES OF STOIC
EMOTIONAL RESILIENCE

Stoic emotional resilience can be easily illustrated in the following examples.

Antonine Plague
As emperor, Marcus Aurelius led Rome through the Antonine Plague, which killed millions. Despite personal grief and immense public pressure, he remained a model of composure and duty. Because he understood that there were forces and events outside of his control, he focused on what he *could* control—his own rational decision-making and emotional steadiness. He reminded himself that strength was attainable through keeping his focus on his thoughts, not on external forces.

Seneca's Exile
Seneca was unjustly exiled to Corsica. Rather than succumbing to despair, he used the time for philosophical writing and reflection, embracing Stoic acceptance and emotional resilience in the face of adversity.

EMOTIONAL RESILIENCE
IN EVERYDAY LIFE

Practicing Stoic emotional resilience in your personal life may help you to deal with the stress and uncertainty of life. By not allowing your emotions to override your rationality, you can easily take things in stride. Now, the Stoics did not ask people to avoid their emotions but to rationally manage them. In fact, there are times when you *want* to feel what are considered "negative emotions."

For example, when a loved one dies, you want to feel sadness and grieve over the loss. Marcus Aurelius lost many of his children throughout his life and grieved over their deaths, but even in his grief, he did not let it override his ability to govern those under his stewardship. As Seneca aptly explains, "It's better to conquer grief than to deceive it."

Emotions are powerful drivers of human behavior, and the Stoics gave people the tools to deal with them effectively rather than letting them override their better judgment. Managing your emotions and learning to accept or love everything that happens to you will give you the resilience to ride the ups and downs of the vagaries of life.

TECHNIQUES FOR MANAGING EMOTIONS

Tools for Equanimity

Quotable Voices
"When you have been compelled by circumstances to be disturbed in a manner, quickly return to yourself and do not continue out of tune longer than the compulsion lasts."

—Marcus Aurelius

The common things that you struggle with in everyday life can cause you tremendous amounts of stress, anger, sadness, or even grief. But what if you could reduce your amount of suffering while you work through these challenges?

A key reason why Stoicism is such a popular philosophy even today is that it contains a set of robust tools to stay emotionally balanced and maintain inner calm. To practice Stoicism, you can simply focus on learning a few clear and practical ideas, and do your best to consistently apply them in your daily life.

For example, imagine a colleague undermines you in a meeting, and rather than reacting with anger, you're able to take a breath, reflect on the situation, and respond calmly. Later, when you've had time to reflect on the situation, you're able to address the issue rationally or even let it go completely. The Stoics, with their practical wisdom, developed practical tools for just such situations.

STOIC TECHNIQUES FOR EMOTIONAL MANAGEMENT

Emotional management is key for Stoics. The following are some techniques taught in Stoicism.

Negative Visualization

The Stoics felt that much of a person's suffering in life comes from their attachment to external things such as possessions or their reputation. By regularly imagining losing the things you value, you appreciate what you have and prepare emotionally for potential losses. Seneca, in his *Moral Letters to Lucilius*, writes, "He robs present ills of their power who has perceived their coming beforehand." (You can read more about this practice in the later *Premeditatio Malorum* section.)

An example of negative visualization is as follows: If you're worried about an upcoming job interview, you may obsess over every possible negative outcome. A Stoic approach would be to view these outcomes as possible pathways the interview might take, prepare as best as possible to address potential pitfalls, and then accept the outcome, knowing you have done all you can. This allows you to focus on performing well in the present.

Mindfulness and Reflection

The Stoics placed a strong emphasis on taking time each day to reflect on one's thoughts and actions. They argued that because a person's judgments are responsible for their emotions, it's important to be aware of one's thoughts. This way one can decide if those thoughts are useful, or if they should be discarded for more helpful perspectives. By taking time for daily journaling or meditation, you can uncover the source of your discomfort. As Marcus Aurelius aptly observes, "Look well into thyself; there is a source of strength which will always spring up if thou wilt always look."

OBJECTIVE JUDGMENT

Another practice that can help you in mastering your emotions is to focus on objective judgment. Ask yourself if your reaction is based on facts or assumptions. By rationally looking at situations and only paying attention to what can be observed and factually proven, you can notice where your emotions and biases influence your judgments and reactions. Epictetus reminds the astute Stoic that it is judgments, not the events themselves, that upset people.

In the previous example about being undermined by a colleague, an objective way to handle the situation would be to examine the situation and parse out the facts. Did what your colleague say have any truth to it? If so, this might be an area that you might need to improve. Can you discern any motives that would drive them to undermine you? In this case, you may be able to uncover sources of potential friction with this person and use this insight to develop a more productive relationship. By taking time to objectively understand the situation, you can find a more positive way forward while retaining your inner calm.

REFRAMING

While the Stoics often had a reputation for stifling their emotions, this is far from the truth. They understood that humans have emotions, but that people should not let their emotions overwhelm them. By taking the time to understand the thoughts that caused their emotions, Stoics could change their views of a situation, allowing them to change the negative emotions they are feeling and turn them toward a more positive and helpful outcome.

For example, if a Stoic lost a loved one, they would allow themselves to grieve but also reflect on the natural cycle of life and death. By appreciating the time spent with their loved one and focusing on the positive memories, they would gradually move toward acceptance and peace.

The Stoics understood the challenges of being human and dealing with the power of emotions. They also saw the consequences of not handling emotions in a rational and reasonable way. Through their own observations and experiences, Stoics developed techniques to manage emotions in the most productive and useful way possible, all while retaining humanity and a core part of the lived human experience.

THE STOIC RESPONSE TO ANGER, ANXIETY, AND SADNESS

Dealing with Negative Emotions

Quotable Voices

"A man is as unhappy as he has convinced himself he is."

—Seneca

Stoicism offers timeless wisdom for dealing with life's emotional challenges. Anger, anxiety, and sadness are universal experiences that everyone encounters. The Stoic approach to these emotions provides practical strategies for managing them and achieving a state of inner peace.

THE STOIC APPROACH TO ANGER

The Stoics understood that anger is one of the most powerful human emotions, one that can cloud judgment and lead to regrettable actions. Stoicism teaches that anger stems from an incorrect judgment of events and is often an attempt to control things that are outside of one's control, such as the actions of others or external events.

Seneca devoted an entire treatise to the topic, titled *De Ira* (*On Anger*). He writes, "My anger is more likely to do me more harm than your wrong." Because anger is one of the strongest core human emotions, learning to control your anger in the moment can prevent you from making a situation even worse. Seneca advises that "the greatest remedy for anger is delay." Taking time to pause and reflect before reacting in anger, and assessing whether the response is proportional and justified, prevents hasty and destructive actions.

THE STOIC APPROACH TO ANXIETY

When considering the Stoic approach to anxiety, think of the following.

The Future

"The mind that is anxious about future events is miserable," writes Seneca, as a reminder that anxiety often arises from concerns about the future. Mirroring their beliefs about anger, the Stoics believed that anxiety is caused by an error in judgment. They reasoned that the future outcomes a person might worry about are beyond their control and may not even happen, so worrying about these outcomes is a waste of energy. The Stoics emphasized focusing on the present moment and what can be controlled to maintain one's inner peace.

By accepting that you cannot control everything, letting go of your attachment to any particular outcome, and focusing on your own actions and reactions, you can reduce your anxiety over future events. Marcus Aurelius counsels about this, writing, "Whatever happens at all happens as it should; you will find this true, if you watch narrowly."

Contrast with *Premeditatio Malorum*

While the Stoic practice of *Premeditatio Malorum* is all about imagining bad outcomes so one isn't surprised, it should not be confused with worrying over future outcomes. Anxiety about the future focuses on the emotional turmoil over things that may or may not happen, whereas *Premeditatio Malorum* is a calm and rational process of objectively imagining all possible points of failure. For more on this topic, see the *Premeditatio Malorum* section.

The Past

Seneca, in his treatise *On the Shortness of Life*, writes, "Life is divided into three periods, past, present, and future. Of these, the present is short, the future is doubtful, the past is certain." Because the past is already set in stone, holding on to past regrets creates anxiety over something that cannot be changed. The Stoics advised that people learn to accept the past and focus on the present moment. As Epictetus posits, "There is only one way to happiness and that is to cease worrying about things which are beyond the power of our will."

THE STOIC APPROACH TO SADNESS

Sadness, while a natural response to loss and disappointment, can be managed through Stoic practices of rational examination and acceptance. While the Stoics advocated managing one's emotions, these philosophers acknowledged that negative emotions are part of life. However, the Stoics advised against letting negative emotions overwhelm a person to the point where they lose control of themself. There are times that a person would want to feel sadness or grief—such as at the loss of a loved one—but that grief shouldn't overwhelm them and keep them from functioning in daily life.

Marcus Aurelius, who suffered the loss of many of his children, offers a perspective on dealing with sorrow: "Do not be perturbed, for all things are according to the nature of the universal; and in a little time you will be nobody and nowhere, like Hadrian and Augustus." This quote speaks to the transient nature of all things, including a person's life. Keeping this perspective helped Aurelius put sadness into context and focus on the present.

The Stoic response to anger, anxiety, and sadness is grounded in rationality, self-control, and acceptance. By applying Stoic principles, you can better manage your emotions, maintain inner peace, and lead a more fulfilling life. The teachings of Seneca, Epictetus, and Marcus Aurelius provide timeless strategies for dealing with life's challenges and teach that while you cannot always control what happens to you, you can control how you respond.

OIKEIÔSIS

The Stoic Concept of Moral Development

Quotable Voices

"As thou thyself art a component part of a social system, so let every act of thine be a component part of social life."

—Marcus Aurelius

The Stoic concept of *oikeiôsis*, or "affiliation," is a fundamental principle in Stoic ethics; *oikeiôsis* explains the process by which a rational being develops an understanding of self, moral duty, and affection toward others. The term derives from the Greek word *oikos*, meaning "family" or "household." This concept is central to understanding how Stoics perceived ethical development, community, cosmopolitanism, and interpersonal relationships.

Philosophical Definition

cosmopolitanism: The Stoic concept of cosmopolitanism, in Greek *kosmopolitēs*, meaning "citizen of the world," is the idea that rather than viewing a person as belonging to only a small group or community, a person should be seen as belonging to all of humanity.

In *Meditations*, Marcus Aurelius walks through how a person comes to the rational conclusion of cosmopolitanism: "If thought is something we share, then so is reason—what makes us reasoning beings. If so, then the reason that tells us what to do and what not to do is also shared. And if so, we share a common law. And thus, are fellow citizens. And fellow citizens of something. And in that case, our state must be the world."

ORIGINS AND DEVELOPMENT
OF *OIKEIÔSIS*

The concept of *oikeiôsis* initially focuses on the instinctual impulses of self-preservation and care that are evident even in animals. For humans, this natural inclination starts with a concern for one's own survival and well-being but gradually extends to the welfare of others as reason and moral awareness develop.

STAGES OF *OIKEIÔSIS*

Oikeiôsis consists of four distinct stages that tend to correspond with the cognitive development of a human being.

Self-Preservation
The earliest stage of *oikeiôsis* involves the natural inclination toward self-care and preservation. This trait is common to all living beings and serves as the foundation for more complex forms of social affection.

Rational Self-Interest
As human beings mature, they begin to use reason to understand their needs more deeply and recognize that their well-being is tied to their moral character and rational choices, not merely to external conditions. They can make individual choices and take actions to get their needs met.

Social Affection
The next stage of *oikeiôsis* involves extending care beyond a person to their family and close friends. This is driven by the realization

that others also have similar needs and desires for happiness and well-being, and that by working together, they can help meet their needs and the needs of others.

Moral Awareness and Universal Concern

At its most developed stage, *oikeiôsis* leads to a concern for the well-being of all rational beings. The Stoics argued that as a person's understanding of the nature of the self expands, so does their affinity for and ethical obligation toward all humanity. The Stoic idea of cosmopolitanism emerges from a broad application of *oikeiôsis*.

PHILOSOPHICAL IMPLICATIONS

The philosophical implications of *oikeiôsis* are to help people to see how they can enlarge their definition of family, expanding from their natural family to the rest of humanity, and see themselves as part of the cosmos.

The Human Family

While direct quotes on *oikeiôsis* are less common in Stoicism's surviving texts, the principle is implicit in many Stoic teachings. Hierocles, a Stoic philosopher, illustrated the concept with his famous image of concentric circles. The self is at the center, surrounded by family, then community, and finally all humanity. He advised drawing the circles closer together, effectively treating all human beings as part of their own family. By expanding your circle of who you consider part of your family, you are better able to extend compassion and empathy to all of humanity, rather than just focusing on your own narrow self-interest or those closest to you.

Oikeiôsis in the Development of Virtue

Oikeiôsis is crucial for understanding Stoic ethics because it underpins the development of virtues and the Stoic commitment to justice and universal love. Stoics believed that, by nature, humans are rational and social beings, and thus, they are naturally predisposed to form communities and live cooperatively. The concept of *oikeiôsis* emphasizes empathy, ethical behavior in society, and global citizenship. It encourages viewing others' interests as interconnected with one's own, thus promoting a more cooperative and empathetic approach to social and global challenges.

Oikeiôsis and the *Logos*

Oikeiôsis is also intertwined with the Stoic concept of the *Logos*, that there is a purposeful and benevolent structure to the cosmos. Marcus Aurelius reflects on this in *Meditations*, writing, "The world as a living being—one nature, one soul. Keep that in mind. . . . And how everything helps produce everything else. Spun and woven together." Because the Stoics believed that every person is a part of nature, and that everyone should treat all beings with compassion and empathy as part of living according to nature. For more on the concept of the *Logos*, see The *Logos* section.

Oikeiôsis encapsulates the Stoic vision of moral development and social ethics, explaining the progression from personal survival to rational self-interest, and ultimately to a universal concern for all rational beings. Increasing a person's circle of who they consider part of their family beautifully illustrates how Stoicism is both a personal and social philosophy, deeply committed to fostering ethical living and mutual respect among all people.

COMPASSION AND EMPATHY IN STOICISM

The Stoic Heart

Quotable Voices
"Life is short—the fruit of this life is a
good character and acts for the common good."
—Marcus Aurelius

While Stoicism advocates for the rational control of emotions, it does not mean that Stoics are heartless automatons. This view of Stoicism is due to the common misconception that it promotes emotional detachment or indifference. In fact, the Stoics felt that how a person treats others is so important that they included justice as one of the four cardinal virtues.

The Stoic virtue of justice isn't just regarding legal frameworks and laws but also relates to how one treats other people in everyday and public life. Stoics felt that it was important to respond with compassion and empathy to the suffering of others because, in doing so, one creates more social harmony and strengthens social bonds.

OIKEIÔSIS

The Stoic concept of *oikeiôsis*, or affiliation, is crucial to understanding how the Stoics viewed and practiced empathy and compassion toward others. This concept starts out with the idea of basic instinctual concern with self-preservation seen in all animals, moving to rational self-interest in the early stages of life. Later, as a person matures, this concern moves outward toward members of their family and close friends, and eventually to all humanity and to that person adopting the idea of cosmopolitanism, meaning seeing themselves as a "citizen of the world." For a deeper dive into *oikeiôsis* and cosmopolitanism, see its earlier section.

COMPASSION IN STOIC PHILOSOPHY

"What is not good for the swarm is not good for the bee," writes Marcus Aurelius. This means that if a person's actions are unhelpful or destructive to society, then they are bad for the individual too. Throughout his reign as Roman emperor, Aurelius used his position and the resources of the government to invest in programs for the poor and for the rehabilitation of soldiers injured in battle. He also helped society by selling some of his own possessions to raise funds for those devastated by the plague that struck his empire in 165 C.E.

Compassion in Stoicism is virtue-driven, meaning that you truly want to understand and help the other person, rather than simply having pity on them. True compassion, in the Stoic sense, means wanting what will help alleviate the suffering of others and what will allow them to live a more virtuous life, rather than simply offering platitudes. It's the difference between helping a friend through a breakup by actively being supportive through their sadness, and just feeling bad for them. One is genuine concern for another's well-being and being focused on helping that person, while the other is just an acknowledgment of how you feel about their situation.

THE ROLE OF EMPATHY IN STOICISM

"We have two ears and one mouth so that we can listen twice as much as we speak," says Epictetus. This is his reminder that practicing empathy helps in understanding others' perspectives. Listening to others allows you to consider their motivations and see a situation from another point of view. Likewise, Seneca advises us to be tolerant and try to put ourselves in the other person's shoes: "No one says to himself, 'I myself have done or could have done the thing that is making me angry now'; no one considers the intention of the person who performs the action, but just the action itself." For the Stoics, empathy and understanding the perspective of others was necessary to foster cooperation, strengthen relationships, and build social harmony.

RATIONALITY AND EMOTIONS

Because the Stoics believed that a person's emotions are caused by their perspective, meaning the story a person creates around events (such as the actions of others), they felt it was important that people understand their thinking around any event. The Stoics argued that by not allowing passions—strong or overwhelming emotions—to control one's decisions, people can use reason and rationality in their dealings with others.

Objectivity
The Stoics felt that a person adept at using rationality and keeping their passions at bay could then view things more objectively. This objectivity allows the individual to see things more closely to

what they really are, to deal with the facts of a situation, and to be more rational, rather than letting emotions cloud their judgment.

Ignorance

"If men do rightly what they do, we ought not to be displeased; but if they do not right, it is plain that they do so involuntarily and in ignorance," writes Marcus Aurelius. This was his reminder to himself to be gentle with others, even when they were behaving poorly. The Stoics believed that no one does evil willingly but rather that a person takes a particular action because they think it is in their best interest. When a person can adopt an objective perspective, it allows them to not take things personally and to be empathetic toward another's motives and behaviors.

Stoic compassion and empathy are rooted in a desire for the betterment of the individual and all humankind. Seneca advocates for compassion and empathy toward others when he writes, "Wherever there is a human being, there is an opportunity for kindness." By understanding the concept of *oikeiôsis*, the interconnectedness of humanity, and using your rationality to treat others with compassion and empathy, you can contribute to the betterment of humanity at both a personal and societal level.

THE ROLE OF RATIONALITY IN EMOTIONAL LIFE

Mind over Mood

Quotable Voices

"Why, what is weeping and sighing? A judgment. What is misfortune? A judgment. What are strife, disagreement, fault-finding, accusing, impiety, foolishness? They are all judgments."

—Epictetus

A key part of Stoic philosophy is using rationality and reason for better management of one's emotional life and, as a result, a happier life. You might think of emotions and rationality as being opposites of each other, but the Stoics believed that using rationality helps people to live richer and fuller emotional lives by governing the strongest drivers of their behavior. The Stoics taught that, rather than working toward the cessation or suppression of emotions, people need to understand the causes of their emotions so that they can choose to address the cause rather than the symptom.

NATURE OF EMOTIONS

The Stoics advocated that people need to control their emotions, which starts by understanding the nature of emotions.

Thoughts and Emotions

The Stoics believed that emotions are a result of one's thoughts and judgments about the circumstances and events happening around oneself, rather than just uncontrollable feelings that happen to a person. By changing your perspective, thoughts, and opinions about your circumstances, you can alter your emotional responses to those circumstances.

Emotions Are Not Enemies

Contrary to the popular belief that Stoicism promotes emotional suppression, it encourages the transformation of emotions through rational scrutiny. The goal is not to eliminate emotions but to refine and understand them so that they serve your well-being and virtue.

NEGATIVE EMOTIONS

The Stoics had many ways to approach emotions, such as the following.

Preferable Emotions

While the Stoics advocated for emotional tranquility (*apatheia*), they distinguished between natural and necessary emotions (like caution, wishfulness, and joy) and destructive emotions (like fear, lust, and distress). They taught that some emotions are rational and preferable if they align with virtue. Uncontrolled passions, such as intense anger or overwhelming sadness, are seen as deviations from nature because they contradict the rational part of the human soul.

The Value of Negative Emotions

Stoicism posits that negative emotions can be useful. The Stoics treated negative emotions as red flags and an invitation to dig deeper to understand what that emotion is trying to indicate. For example, the initial feeling of fear can be a prompt to prepare or take precautionary measures. The Stoic skill lies in not letting such emotions escalate to irrational panic or anxiety.

RATIONALITY

Stoics regarded rationality as a fundamental skill necessary for emotional regulation, but how does rationality help to keep emotions in check?

Happiness Without Passion

Stoics argued for a form of happiness that is independent of *pathos* (passions), which is often seen as vital for a fulfilling life in other philosophical or modern psychological approaches. By reducing the sway that negative emotions such as anger, jealousy, and anxiety have on you, you can face the challenges in life through a more positive and productive perspective. The Stoics believed true happiness comes from a harmonious inner rationality and virtue.

Emotional Control Through Reasoning

The Stoics taught that when a person reacts emotionally, then they are letting someone else have control over them. If one allows something that someone said to stir them to anger, then they have given the other power over them.

Because emotions can cause you to see situations with a distorted perspective, making efforts to practice objectivity and view your emotions from a distance give you control over them. Rather than reacting on your first impulse, you can examine your judgments and see if they are valid, and account for any biases or preexisting opinions you might have.

For example, if someone criticizes a piece of art you made, rather than seeing it as a personal attack, you can rationally examine what was said and see if there is any truth to it. If there is truth, then you can decide how you take in this new information. If there is not, then you can try to understand the motivation behind the criticism. In either case, you can limit the control that your emotional response has over you and deal with the situation in a rational and productive way. You may do well to follow the advice of Seneca: "Do battle with yourself: if you have the will to conquer anger, it cannot conquer you."

Epictetus and the Lamp

Epictetus used an example from his own life to illustrate the Stoic idea of how to use rationality to manage emotions: "The other day I had an iron lamp placed beside my household gods. I heard a noise at the door and on hastening down found my lamp carried off. I reflected that the culprit was in no very strange case. 'Tomorrow, my friend,' I said, 'you will find an earthenware lamp; for a man can only lose what he has.'"

Rather than being upset that the thief had stolen his lamp, he used his rationality to decide how he wanted to respond. In this case, he decided that putting himself through the stress and anger trying to track down the thief to get his lamp back wasn't worth it. He decided instead to simply buy himself a cheaper lamp. He goes on to have compassion for the thief: "He acquired the lamp at a price: he became a thief for its sake, for its sake, he lost his ability to be trusted, for a lamp he became a brute. And he imagined he came out ahead."

Rationality is a key skill for Stoics to manage their emotions, rather than being ruled by them. The more you practice rationally interrogating your emotions and the thoughts and judgments behind them, the more you are in charge of yourself rather than being caught in the throes of your emotional reactions to the disappointments and challenges of life.

THE ROLE OF SUFFERING

If It's Endurable, Then Endure It

Quotable Voices
"To bear trials with a calm mind robs misfortune
of its strength and burden."

—Seneca

Life is full of external events over which you have no control. There is a natural tendency within a person to blame the suffering in their lives on things outside of themselves. The Stoics taught that most suffering comes from misjudgments about Externals. The Stoics' perspective on suffering focuses on understanding, accepting, and transcending pain and adversity. This approach to suffering is deeply intertwined with their beliefs in the power of personal resilience and the importance of viewing challenges as opportunities for growth.

STOIC PRINCIPLES ON THE NATURE OF SUFFERING

The Stoics classified external events and circumstances as "indifferents," which are outside of moral good (virtue) and evil (vice). Moral good is defined as living the four virtues of wisdom, courage, justice, and temperance, and moral evil is acting in opposition of virtue.

Externals are neither good nor evil—though they may cause physical suffering—so emotional or mental suffering is caused when a person fails to live with virtue or to control what they can. When people understand what they can control (like their perspective, choices, and actions), they can live the four virtues and reduce their suffering. When they fail due to being ignorant or foolish, acting unjustly, or not practicing temperance, they become the cause of their own suffering.

TRANSFORMING SUFFERING INTO GROWTH

The Stoics taught that suffering is based on one's perceptions and that people can decrease their suffering through reason and rationality. Read on to explore these ideas a little more in depth.

Perception of Suffering

When external events happen, the story and meaning you give them is what causes your suffering. For example, if you are laid off from a job—it's your reaction to that layoff that causes emotional distress. You may think you're a failure, worry about your reputation, or imagine the awful things that might happen because of your job loss. These are all a result of your perspective, not the layoff itself.

Use of Reason

According to the Stoics, using reason allows people to reinterpret and manage their emotional responses to suffering. By reframing the loss of a job through a more rational lens, you can see the event from a neutral perspective. Were you laid off because of financial concerns within the company or because of poor performance? If it's the former, then it is truly outside of your power, and you can begin a search for a new position. If it's the latter, then you can take the job loss as a signal that you need to improve and find ways to upgrade your skills. In both situations, you can identify what you have control over and take action. As Epictetus states, "Make the best use of what is in our power, and treat the rest in accordance with its nature."

PHYSICAL SUFFERING AND STOICISM

Physical suffering is an aspect of life that no one can escape. For the Stoic, recognizing that this suffering is something not to be feared but to be endured well can be a way to strengthen character.

Endurance As a Virtue

Since life is full of challenges, the Stoics placed importance on developing one's endurance for physical discomfort and pain and using that endurance to cultivate virtue. As Marcus Aurelius puts it, "If it is endurable, then endure it. Stop complaining." By bearing unavoidable suffering with composure and dignity, you can develop courage and self-discipline. Through managing your own suffering, you can become more empathetic to the suffering of others. Every hardship you endure is a chance for you to find ways to grow and practice virtue. To read more on the Stoics' ideas about endurance, see the Stoicism and the Role of Physical Exercise and Discipline section.

Examples from the Stoics

Stoics often persevered in the face of physical hardships. Seneca was reported to have suffered from several illnesses, including asthma and possibly tuberculosis, making breathing difficult and often painful. Cleanthes, successor to Zeno of Citium as the head of the Stoic school, was so poor that he worked nightly as a water carrier, a physically demanding job, to support his study of philosophy. Marcus Aurelius suffered from poor health, including stomach issues and recurrent chest pains that made tending to his administrative duties difficult. Epictetus suffered from a limp for most of his life after his leg was broken by his master in a fit of rage. In each case of physical adversity, the Stoics used them as opportunities to develop their inner resolve.

Whether a person suffers from physical pain/discomfort or internal struggles, the Stoics saw both as ways to develop virtue. Epictetus explains this clearly:

"Every difficulty in life presents us with an opportunity to turn inward and to invoke our own inner resources. The trials we endure can and should introduce us to our strengths. Prudent people look beyond the incident itself and seek to form the habit of putting it to good use. On the occasion of an accidental event, don't just react in a haphazard fashion: remember to turn inward and ask what resources you have for dealing with it. Dig deeply. You possess strengths you might not realize you have. Find the right one. Use it."

—Epictetus

Every setback, including physical pain and suffering, is an opportunity for personal growth and a chance to discover how strong you truly are.

AMOR FATI

The Stoic Concept of Embracing Life

Quotable Voices

"Here is your great soul—the man who has given himself over to Fate; on the other hand, that man is a weakling and a degenerate who struggles and maligns the order of the universe and would rather reform the gods than reform himself."

—Seneca

One of the most profound and life-affirming concepts of Stoic wisdom is *Amor Fati*. This Stoic principle surpasses a resignation to fate; it is about falling in love with whatever life throws at you, seeing the necessity of events, and internalizing everything that happens as essential.

This concept is beautifully expressed by Friedrich Nietzsche, who, though not a Stoic himself, echoed Stoic principles when he wrote, "My formula for greatness in a human being is *amor fati*: that one wants nothing to be different, not forward, not backward, not in all eternity. Not merely bear what is necessary, still less conceal it . . . but love it."

Philosophical Definition

Amor Fati: A Latin phrase that translates to "love of fate" or "love of one's fate." This Stoic concept means that a person should not just accept their circumstances but embrace them with enthusiasm, regardless of their nature.

STOIC FOUNDATIONS OF *AMOR FATI*

While the term itself was popularized by Nietzsche, the concept is deeply rooted in Stoic philosophy. Stoic thinkers like Marcus Aurelius, Seneca, and Epictetus often expressed ideas that closely align with *Amor Fati*. The Stoics believed that while external circumstances are outside of one's control, one's responses are under one's control. So, rather than resisting things external to oneself, one should embrace them as opportunities for growth and cultivating virtue.

In *Meditations*, Marcus Aurelius writes about accepting one's fate: "Whatever happens to you has been waiting to happen since the beginning of time. The twining strands of fate wove both of them together: your own existence and the things that happen to you." Aurelius felt that one should embrace what happens and do one's best with the hand fate has dealt.

AMOR FATI IN PRACTICE

Throughout time, there have been powerful examples of how the concept of *Amor Fati* has been used to turn difficult and challenging circumstances into opportunities to practice virtue and make a greater impact on humanity.

Epictetus

Epictetus himself was a potent example of practicing *Amor Fati*. Born enslaved, Epictetus faced immense hardships, including being deliberately crippled by his master. Yet, rather than resenting his fate, Epictetus embraced his circumstances and used them to forge his philosophical outlook. He taught that happiness stems from aligning one's desires with whatever happens, which is the essence of *Amor Fati*. He states, "Whoever chafes at the conditions dealt by fate is unskilled in the art of life; whoever bears with them nobly and makes wise use of the results is a man who deserves to be considered good."

Nelson Mandela

In modern times, you can look to the life of Nelson Mandela as an example of the Stoic practice of *Amor Fati*. Mandela's twenty-seven years in prison could have been viewed as a tragic waste. Instead, he embraced his fate, using the time to grow intellectually and spiritually, ultimately preparing him to lead South Africa with wisdom and empathy.

THE POWER OF *AMOR FATI*

Amor Fati is not a passive acceptance of the challenges and trials that life brings but rather a way for a person to choose their own perceptions about things outside of their control. While the Stoics believed in the deterministic nature of the cosmos, the *Logos*, they believed that a person could choose to respond to the external events and circumstances of life, and part of that is to intentionally pick one's attitude toward what happens in life.

Adopting *Amor Fati* as a lens through which to view life transforms how you approach challenges. It helps you to view life's circumstances as things not just to be tolerated but to be celebrated. *Amor Fati* encourages a joyful acceptance of all experiences, turning obstacles into opportunities for growth. The challenges you face are the things that help you develop the skills to become a stronger person, so you should be grateful for them. This mindset can dramatically reduce personal suffering because it eliminates the struggle against the inevitable, changes the resentment of undesirable situations, and alters the view of adversity, making it a catalyst for greatness. As Seneca aptly puts it: "The bravest sight in the world is to see a great man struggling against adversity."

Amor Fati is not simply seeing the world through rose-colored glasses; it's an acknowledgment that you can't control external events and circumstances. It's a manifestation of the Dichotomy of Control, in that you cannot control what happens to you, but you can choose your perspectives and your responses. By choosing to "love your fate," you are choosing to view everything that happens to you as something that can be used for good.

Amor Fati is a Stoic practice that promotes a powerful and positive engagement with life. It teaches that a person who loves their fate, rather than resenting it, gains an unshakeable strength and tranquility. In the words of Marcus Aurelius, "Everything suits me that suits your designs, O my universe!" *Amor Fati* is not a passive surrender but an active celebration of life. By embracing every moment and challenge as necessary, you align yourself with the cosmos and find peace in the unavoidable flow of life.

STOICISM'S INFLUENCE ON CHRISTIAN ETHICS

A Philosophical Intersection

Quotable Voices

"You need not look about for the reward of a just deed;
a just deed in itself offers a still greater return."

—Seneca

Stoic philosophy, which flourished in Greece and Rome from the third century B.C.E. until the third century C.E., had a profound influence on subsequent philosophical and religious traditions, including Christian ethics. Stoic thought, with its assertion that virtue leads to happiness and its focus on the development of self-control and fortitude, had a significant impact on early Christian moral teachings. They overlapped in many areas of ethical thought.

THE OVERLAP OF STOICISM AND CHRISTIAN ETHICS

Stoicism and Christian ethics were seen as having areas of confluence, meaning places where they overlapped. Here are a few examples.

Emphasis on Universal Love and Brotherhood

Stoic thought was distinguished by cosmopolitanism, the idea that all people are manifestations of the one universal spirit (*Logos*), and that they should live in brotherly love and readily help one another. In *Meditations*, Marcus Aurelius sums up the Stoic vision of a unified humanity: "My city and state are Rome—as Antoninus. But as a human being? The world. So for me, 'good' can only mean what's good for both communities."

Stoicism's cosmopolitanism seamlessly blends with the Christian commandment of love. Both philosophies advocate for love as a duty toward all humankind, transcending local affiliations and personal prejudices. Musonius Rufus, a Stoic philosopher and contemporary of the Stoic Epictetus, writes, "A virtuous person displays love for his fellow human beings, as well as goodness, justice, kindness, and concern for his neighbor." This directive was later seen in Christianity and echoed by Jesus Christ when he taught "Love your neighbor as yourself" (Matthew 22:39).

Inner Freedom and Moral Autonomy

The Stoic concept of inner freedom through mastery over one's passions is demonstrated in Christian teachings on self-control and resisting worldly temptations. "For what does it profit a man to gain the whole world and forfeit his soul?" (Mark 8:36) parallels Stoic warnings against external temptations disrupting a person's moral integrity.

Endurance of Suffering

Stoicism's emphasis on endurance and resilience in the face of hardship is seen within the Christian ideal of suffering for faith and moral integrity. Stoic Seneca writes, "Fire tests gold, suffering tests brave men." In Christianity, the suffering of martyrs who stood firm in their faith is held in high esteem, as seen in Hebrews 12:1: "Let us run with perseverance the race marked out for us."

INFLUENCE AND INTEGRATION

There were central figures who supported the overlap of Stoicism and Christianity, including the following.

Justin Martyr

The early Christian thinker Justin Martyr had at one point studied to become a Stoic philosopher and acknowledged that the Stoics held views that were remarkably similar to Christian teachings, suggesting a divine influence in the moral teachings of the Stoics.

Tertullian

Tertullian, an early Christian writer, though critical of pagan philosophies, quoted the Stoic Seneca and referred to him as one "whom we so often find on our side" and as "our Seneca." Attempting to make Christianity more palatable to a Stoic-minded audience, he appropriated Stoic concepts such as living according to virtue and self-discipline as a means to be closer to God.

Saint Ambrose

Saint Ambrose, Bishop of Milan, a prominent theologian and statesman throughout the fourth century C.E., was raised studying Stoic philosophy, which was common among the aristocratic families of the time. His works are known to have been influenced by Stoic philosophy, particularly in his ethical writings.

Seneca

The early Christian Church was very favorable toward Seneca. By the fourth century C.E., a set of letters supposedly of a correspondence between Seneca and Paul the Apostle had been created, linking Seneca to the Christian tradition. Though the letters have since been shown to be inauthentic, the church's previous acceptance shows its early efforts to define itself in harmony with Stoic and Greco-Roman teachings and intellectual traditions.

DIVERGENCE IN THEOLOGICAL UNDERPINNINGS

Though they have a lot of overlap, Christianity and Stoicism are fundamentally different for the following reasons.

Metaphysics

Despite some similarities, Christianity and Stoicism diverge in their theological and metaphysical foundations. Christianity is a monotheistic religion that centers on the teachings, resurrection, and divine nature of Jesus Christ, emphasizing faith and God's grace as the means to salvation. In contrast, Stoicism is pantheistic and focuses on personal and ethical improvement as ends in themselves, guided by rationality and reason.

The *Logos* and Jesus

The Stoic concept of the *Logos*, which comes from the Greek for "word" or "reason," is the divine, animating principle of the universe. The *Logos* orders and defines the structure of the cosmos, ensuring that the universe operates in a purposeful manner. In Christian theology, Jesus is the "Word" (*Logos*) made flesh, who was sent to dwell among humanity and becomes the means of their salvation. For the Stoics, the *Logos* is distant and unknowable, whereas Christianity highlights an importance of having a personal relationship with God and Jesus Christ. For more on the *Logos*, see its section earlier in the book.

The intersection between Stoicism and Christian ethics highlights a significant philosophical and theological exchange. Stoic ideas helped shape early Christian thoughts on love, endurance, and ethical living, having a significant impact on Christian ethical traditions. This blending of ideas from Stoicism and Christianity illustrates a profound dialogue between Greco-Roman philosophy and emerging Christian doctrine, both of which have continued to influence ethical thought up to the present day.

The connections between Stoicism and Christian ethics not only enhance modern understanding of early Christian thought; they also offer enduring lessons on the universal challenges of living a moral life. The influence of ancient Stoic concepts on early Christian thinkers shows that the quest for virtue and meaning transcends cultural boundaries, providing timeless guidance for ethical conduct and personal growth.

STOICISM AND MODERN PSYCHOLOGY

Cognitive Behavioral Therapy and Other Modern Therapies

Quotable Voices

"We are more often frightened than hurt; and we suffer more from imagination than from reality."

—Seneca

With its focus on understanding the root of human suffering and how to live a good and happy life, Stoicism has profoundly influenced modern psychology and its therapeutic practices. While there are many factors to a person's mental health, such as biology, circumstances, and general disposition, Stoicism can be useful in helping people deal with the regular ups and downs of life.

MODERN COGNITIVE THERAPIES

Stoicism is seen and applied often in the following types of modern cognitive therapies.

Cognitive Behavioral Therapy (CBT)

One of the most direct influences of Stoicism on modern psychology is seen in CBT. Aaron T. Beck, one of the founders of CBT, stated, "The philosophical origins of cognitive therapy can be traced back to the Stoic philosophers." CBT's foundational principle that one's thoughts influence one's feelings and behaviors echoes Epictetus's assertion that a person is upset by their own judgments of something that happens rather than by the event itself.

Rational Emotive Behavior Therapy (REBT)

Developed by Albert Ellis, REBT—a precursor to CBT—shares the Stoic idea that emotional disturbances come from irrational beliefs and that changing these beliefs through logical and empirical questioning can lead to better emotional outcomes. Ellis attributed the central tenant of REBT, that people are rarely emotionally affected by external events but by the thoughts regarding those events, to the Stoic philosophers. He often cited Stoic philosophers to support his therapy's principles, demonstrating how ancient Stoic concepts are applied in modern psychological practices.

Acceptance and Commitment Therapy (ACT)

ACT differs from CBT and REBT in that, while the others focus on cognitively challenging one's thoughts to change one's outlook and behavior, ACT focuses on helping a person understand what is under their control. This form of therapy incorporates Stoic principles by teaching clients to accept what is out of their personal control and to commit to action that enriches their life, reflecting the Stoic emphasis on accepting fate and pursuing virtue.

COUNTERINTUITIVE IDEAS

These groundbreaking therapies tended to go against conventional wisdom of psychological understanding of their time. Even though many of the ideas contained in these therapies are based on Stoic ideas and principles that were taught over two thousand years ago, they were overtaken by other religious ideologies or simply forgotten over time. The reintroduction of these ideas in modern data-driven approaches shows the value of the Stoics' timeless wisdom in navigating the challenges of life in any era.

Emotions As Choices

One of the key ideas that Stoicism posits that runs counter to much of modern thinking is that emotions are not just happenstances but are the result of one's judgments and choices, and that negative emotions are caused by one's misjudgments of situations. This idea is counterintuitive in a modern context where emotions are often viewed as automatic or uncontrollable. Therapies like CBT and REBT work to help a person understand that they are not at the whims of external circumstances in managing their emotional states, and that they can take actions to deal with their emotions productively.

The Value of Negative Emotions

In modern times, people tend to look at negative emotions as something that is a hindrance to their happiness. They often try to remove them from their daily life by trying to ignore them or numb them by external means such as drugs or alcohol, or by acquiring wealth and fame. Both Stoicism and modern therapies like CBT do not aim to eliminate negative emotions but rather propose that such emotions, when based on rational and accurate perceptions, can serve valuable purposes, such as motivating change.

STOIC PRACTICES IN
MODERN PSYCHOLOGY

Stoicism is often used in modern psychology, like in the following examples.

Negative Visualization

Many modern psychological practices sometimes incorporate the Stoic exercise of negative visualization (*Premeditatio Malorum*), imagining the worst-case scenario to reduce anxiety about it. In doing so, patients can face their fears more directly and find constructive ways to deal with them. To read more about Stoic negative visualization, see the *Premeditatio Malorum* section.

View from Above

The "view from above," whereby a person gains perspective by imagining their life from a broader context, is another Stoic practice that is used in modern psychology. Often, you get so focused on your own problems you end up stuck in rumination and catastrophizing, causing stress and anxiety. By helping patients to see themselves as part of a larger whole, connected to others who have the same worries and obstacles, practitioners help patients to reframe their perspective and see their problems as being small when compared to the whole of humanity. For more on this practice, see The Stoic "View from Above" section.

Stoicism influenced and continues to resonate within modern psychological practices, providing a robust framework for understanding human behavior and emotional regulation. The practical and timeless principles taught by Stoic philosophers have had a profound impact on humanity by reducing suffering and creating lasting change in the lives of countless people.

THE CRITIQUE OF STOICISM

Misconceptions and Limitations

Quotable Voices

"If someone can prove me wrong and show me my mistake in any thought or action, I shall gladly change. I seek the truth, which never harmed anyone: the harm is to persist in one's own self-deception and ignorance."

—Marcus Aurelius

While Stoicism is a powerful set of principles used to live a good life, it's important to take a critical examination of its misconceptions and limitations. The Stoic tradition evolved from the ancient study of philosophers like Plato and Socrates, who used questions to establish the truth; in the same way, earnestly questioning Stoic tenets may lead to a greater understanding.

MISCONCEPTIONS ABOUT STOICISM

Many people misunderstand certain aspects of Stoicism. The following are several examples.

Emotionlessness

Probably the most common misconception about Stoicism is that the Stoics advocated for the suppression or elimination of emotions. According to the *American Heritage Dictionary of the English Language*, the term *stoic* is defined as "one who is seemingly indifferent to or unaffected by joy, grief, pleasure, or pain." However, Stoics aimed to manage and rationalize emotions to prevent irrational and harmful reactions, not to become devoid of feeling.

Part of the reason behind this misconception comes from a Stoic's ability to remain calm in otherwise emotionally charged situations. When others might react strongly, because a Stoic has practiced keeping their cool and managing their emotional responses, a Stoic's rationality can often be seen as being emotionless and cold.

As an example, modern interpretations of Stoicism often emphasize its relevance to leadership, focusing on emotional regulation and ethical consistency. However, people may then see these Stoic leaders as unemotional or overly detached. Rather than being emotionless, a Stoic feels their emotion and intentionally responds in what they think is the most productive way possible.

Perceived Passivity

Stoicism is sometimes criticized for promoting passivity because of its emphasis on accepting things outside one's control. Critics argue that this can lead to complacency, especially in situations where change is possible and desirable. However, the Stoics argued that people should accept things that they have no control over but also that they should take action where they can in any situation. Doing so increases the probability that one's actions and choices will be more effective.

Contentment

Similar to accepting one's fate, the Stoic idea of being content with what one has and limiting one's desires has also been criticized for promoting passivity. The argument is that if you are completely content with what you already have and you've limited your desires, then there is no willingness to strive and achieve goals.

On the contrary, the Stoics taught the limiting of desires because they understood that outcomes are unpredictable and placing one's happiness on a particular result leads to unhappiness and discontentment. By focusing on being present and enjoying the journey, you will find more contentment and accept the outcome whatever it might be. As Epictetus teaches, "So when you hear that even life and the like are indifferent, don't become apathetic."

LIMITATIONS OF STOICISM

Everything has its limits (even Stoicism). Here are some examples of where this philosophy loses ground.

Overemphasis on Rationality

Stoicism's heavy emphasis on living according to rationality and logic can sometimes dismiss the value and insights derived from non-rational sources such as emotions, intuition, or cultural traditions. Epictetus states:

"Since reason is what analyzes and coordinates everything, it should not go itself unanalyzed. Then what will it be analyzed by? Obviously by itself or something different. Now, this something different must either be reason or something superior to reason—which is impossible, since there is nothing superior to reason."

—Epictetus

While rationality generally leads to more consistent decision-making, it can result in decisions that, while logical, may lack compassion.

Intuition

Sometimes a person finds that seemingly irrational decisions that "feel right" often turn out to be the best course of action. The human mind and its ability to unconsciously recognize patterns, such as the body language of others, might be better served when combined with Stoic rationality, rather than being dismissed out of hand.

Modern Relevance and Practicality

While Stoic principles provide guidance for personal resilience and inner peace, critics argue that it doesn't fully translate to modern societal and technological complexities. For example, in the field of biotechnology, there are many ethical gray areas that are hard to reconcile with Stoicism's ideas of right and wrong. With the advent of AI, there are aspects where Stoicism may fall short as people grapple with an intelligence that may not have the same behaviors or the same values as humans.

Rationality and the *Logos*

Many modern Stoics, while appreciating Stoicism's focus on rationality, disregard its theology, especially the *Logos*. The Stoics developed the concept of the *Logos* to reconcile some of the intangible questions of life such as "Why are we here?" and "Why do things happen as they do?" Many feel that the *Logos* is not a rational principle and believe that it should not be a part of modern Stoic teachings.

Stoicism is not a panacea for all the challenges of life but rather a far-reaching framework for how to live an ethical and good life. By understanding Stoicism's limitations when applied in contemporary settings, people can still use its universal and timeless principles as a basis for developing nuanced decision-making within modern life.

MEMENTO MORI

You May Leave Life at Any Moment

Quotable Voices

"You could leave life right now.
Let that determine what you do and say and think."

—Marcus Aurelius

Stoicism offers people many rational tools to develop their virtue and sense of well-being. However, one of the most counterintuitive ideas is that of pondering one's own death. This tool, *Memento Mori*, serves to cultivate perspective, prioritize life, and value the present.

Philosophical Definition

Memento Mori: A Latin phrase meaning "remember that you must die." It is a philosophical reminder of the inevitability of death. This concept is a central theme in Stoicism and other philosophical traditions.

THE STOIC PERSPECTIVE ON DEATH

Stoics had a unique perspective on death, breaking it into many different related concepts like the following.

Motivation

Far from being a morbid obsession with death, the Stoics used the reminder of death as a motivation to live more fully, virtuously, and with a sense of urgency. Remembering death is a tool to focus your daily efforts on the important things. Seneca urges, "As each day arises, welcome it as the very best day of all, and make it your own possession. We must seize what flees."

Being in the Present Moment

Remembering death sharpens your senses. It helps you to be more present in your daily life and spend less time living for an uncertain future. When you recognize that all the plans and goals that you have might never happen, you learn to not let your happiness be dependent on the future.

Gratitude

Memento Mori is also a reminder for practicing gratitude, appreciating the fact that you are alive, and savoring the present moment. It's also a reminder to be grateful for what you have, rather than waiting for some future event or accomplishment. As Seneca says, "When a man has said: 'I have lived!', every morning he arises he receives a bonus."

Overcoming the Fear of Death

Epictetus says, "I cannot escape death, but at least I can escape the fear of it." This teaches the importance of living in accordance with nature and accepting that death is inevitable. Death isn't a thing to be feared but to be understood and accepted. Epictetus even pokes fun at a person's fear of and their need to accept death, quipping, "Death is necessary and cannot be avoided. I mean, where am I going to go to get away from it?"

Marcus Aurelius advises going a step further: "Think of yourself as dead. You have lived your life. Now, take what's left and live it properly." By imagining that you have already died and are living on borrowed time, you focus on living your best life.

PRACTICAL APPLICATIONS OF
MEMENTO MORI

Practical applications of *Memento Mori* appear in many ways, like the following.

Daily Awareness

The Stoics recommended keeping the inevitability of death in mind in order to forget about the unimportant things and focus on what truly matters. Remembering the temporary nature of life, you're less likely to waste time. "Do not act as if you had ten thousand years to throw away. Death stands at your elbow. Be good for something while you live and it is in your power," writes Marcus Aurelius as an admonition to live well since every day could be his last.

Ethical Living

Remembering death encourages you to consider the legacy you wish to leave behind. This reflection leads to more ethical decisions and actions, as you're constantly aware that each act could be your last. As Seneca advised Lucilius, "Let us prepare our minds as if we'd come to the very end of life. Let us postpone nothing. Let us balance life's books each day. . . . The one who puts the finishing touches on their life each day is never short of time." Reflecting on your mortality each day reinforces the importance of living each day ethically and in a way you wish to be remembered.

Place in History

Memento Mori is also an exercise for recognizing that the things you often worry about and mistakes you've made, when seen through a long time frame, seem insignificant. Marcus Aurelius gives a powerful example of this, writing, "Alexander the Great and his mule driver both died and the same thing happened to both." At the end of the day, whether someone achieves greatness or remains unknown, everyone arrives at the same end.

MODERN EXAMPLES OF *MEMENTO MORI*

Explore several modern purveyors of *Memento Mori* with the following examples.

Steve Jobs

Steve Jobs, cofounder of Apple, famously used *Memento Mori* as a motivational tool. In his 2005 Stanford commencement speech, he mentioned, "Remembering that I'll be dead soon is the most important tool I've ever encountered to help me make the big choices in life." Jobs explained that this awareness helped him to overcome fear of failure and prioritize his true desires, driving him to live each day with purpose.

James Stockdale

Vice Admiral James Stockdale, a modern practitioner of Stoicism, used the principle of *Memento Mori* during his captivity in the Vietnam War. By facing each day as possibly being his last, he was able to endure torture and solitary confinement with strength and courage, fortified by his Stoic beliefs.

Memento Mori remains a powerful Stoic practice. It is about living not with a fear of death but with an awareness and acceptance of death's inevitability that sharpens your focus on living authentically and virtuously. By remembering death, you find a deeper appreciation for life.

PRESENCE AND MINDFULNESS

A Guide to Living Intentionally

Quotable Voices

"You live as if you were destined to live forever, no thought of your frailty ever enters your head, of how much time has already gone by you take no heed. You squander time as if you drew from a full and abundant supply, though all the while that day which you bestow on some person or thing is perhaps your last."

—Seneca

Stoic philosophy focuses on how to live a good life by learning to control what is within one's power and releasing what is not. Stoicism argues that people have control over their perspectives, meaning they have control over how they view things and how they internalize them. Understanding this, the Stoics reasoned that people could learn to be happy wherever they are and whatever situation they find themselves in.

This awareness of your thinking and perspective allows you to eliminate thoughts that lead to negative or undesirable emotions and therefore increase your sense of well-being. As Seneca explains, "A man thus grounded must, whether he wills or not, necessarily be attended by constant cheerfulness and a joy that is deep and issues from deep within, since he finds delight in his own resources, and desires no joys greater than his inner joys."

STOIC PRINCIPLES OF MINDFULNESS

Stoicism teaches that one's thoughts and reactions to external events, not the events themselves, determine one's well-being. Because the future is uncertain, and so much of what shapes what will happen is out of your control, you should concentrate your mental energies on the here and now where you have the most influence. "Confine yourself to the present," penned Marcus Aurelius, encouraging himself to focus on the present moment since the past is unchangeable and the future uncertain.

STOIC PRACTICES FOR ENHANCING MINDFULNESS

Stoics have many different practices for enhancing mindfulness, like the following.

Mindful Reflection

Seneca advises: "When the light has been removed and my wife has fallen silent, aware of this habit that's now mine, I examine my entire day and go back over what I've done and said, hiding nothing from myself, passing nothing by." By taking time for reflection each day, a person is better able to be aware of their own thoughts and perspectives, and ensure they align with Stoic virtue. The Stoics reasoned that if someone is unaware of their thoughts, then they are more likely to be reactive in stressful situations rather than choosing their responses and maintaining their equanimity. For more on reflection, see the Morning and Evening Reflections section.

Objective Observation

Marcus Aurelius practiced viewing life events objectively, without letting emotions cloud his judgment. This detachment is a form of mindfulness that allows for clearer thinking and decision-making. He writes in *Meditations*, "Objective judgment, now, at this very moment. Unselfish action, now, at this very moment. Willing acceptance—now, at this very moment—of all external events. That's all you need."

Contemplation of Death

Stoics frequently contemplated the transient nature of life, a practice known as *Memento Mori*—a Latin phrase meaning "remember that you must die." Contemplating that you will die one day fosters an acute awareness of the impermanence of everything and enhances the appreciation of life's moments.

Practicing Gratitude

Taking the time to regularly acknowledge what you're grateful for shifts focus from what is lacking to what is abundantly present. "When you arise in the morning, think of what a precious privilege it is to be alive—to breathe, to think, to enjoy, to love," penned Marcus Aurelius. This statement was a simple reminder to appreciate his life.

BENEFITS OF MINDFULNESS

There are many great benefits of mindfulness, such as the following.

Reduced Anxiety

Much of a person's anxiety stems from focusing too much on the future for their happiness, rather than being in the present moment. Marcus Aurelius understood this and reminded himself, "Never let the future disturb you. You will meet it, if you have to, with the same weapons of reason which today arm you against the present."

Reduced Distractions

When a person can practice mindfulness and focus on being present, they can avoid distractions more easily. As emperor of Rome, Marcus Aurelius was under constant pressure with the demands of running an empire. Even so, he reminded himself to focus on the task at hand with virtue and diligence, writing, "Concentrate every minute [...] on doing what's in front of you with precise and genuine seriousness, tenderly, willingly, with justice. And on freeing yourself from all other distractions."

Mindful Responses

When a person is fully present, they are more deliberate and engaged with what is going on around them. Rather than simply reacting to stress or provocation, a person who is mindful and present can pause and choose responses governed by reason and virtue, not emotion. As Musonius Rufus states, "The lamp of wisdom shines brightest when lit by the flame of self-awareness."

Emotional Resilience

By focusing on the present and maintaining an objective view, Stoicism helps with cultivating a strong defense against distress and negative emotions. Mindfulness in Stoicism also leads to more ethical and thoughtful behavior, as you're constantly aware of the moral dimensions of your actions.

Stoic philosophy offers timeless wisdom on the importance of mindfulness and living in the present. By embracing Stoic practices, you can cultivate a peaceful mind, live more ethically, and enhance your enjoyment of life. The teachings of the Stoics provide a blueprint for living with intention and a reminder that mindfulness is not merely a modern trend but a universal principle for a well-lived life.

STOICISM IN PERSONAL DEVELOPMENT AND SELF-HELP

A Timeless Guide to Inner Strength

Quotable Voices

"You can pass your life in an equable flow of happiness if you can
follow the right way and think and act in the right way."

—Marcus Aurelius

In recent years, Stoicism has resurged as a philosophy that offers
robust tools for personal development and self-help. Its principles
are rooted in the teachings of ancient philosophers like Zeno, Seneca, Epictetus, and Marcus Aurelius. Stoicism emphasizes resilience,
emotional control, and rational thinking—traits that are highly valuable in contemporary life. With its timeless teachings, Stoicism can
be applied to foster personal growth, improve emotional intelligence,
and enhance overall life satisfaction.

CORE PRINCIPLES OF STOICISM

Stoicism is a practical philosophy and teaches that while an individual cannot always control external events, they can control their
reactions to them. It encourages viewing challenges as opportunities for growth and learning. Statesman and Stoic philosopher
Seneca succinctly captures this idea: "The important thing about a
problem is not its solution, but the strength we gain in finding the
solution." By shifting focus from external events and circumstances

to internal strength and resilience, this mindset is empowering for personal development.

While Stoics advocated a rational and reasoned approach to life, students of Stoicism see through the Stoics' experiences and writings that they struggled with maintaining their equanimity. A clear example of this comes from Marcus Aurelius and his *Meditations*, his own personal journal, which was not meant for publication. You can see throughout his writings that he consistently reminds himself to live a life of virtue, focus on what he could control, and not be unduly influenced by external events.

PRACTICAL APPLICATIONS OF STOICISM IN EVERYDAY LIFE

There are many applications of Stoicism in everyday life, like the following.

Emotional Regulation

With its focus on rationality and reason, Stoicism provides tools for managing one's emotions. The Stoics believed in observing one's emotions objectively, understanding their origins, and then deciding if they are rational or not. Epictetus taught his students that people are upset by their perceptions of things, not the actual thing itself. Applying this concept, you should step back during a stressful event and analyze your emotional response, asking whether your reaction is productive, and how it might be recalibrated to help achieve a better outcome.

Focus on What You Can Control

A central tenet of Stoicism is focusing on what is within one's control—mainly one's thoughts, intentions, and actions. "You have power over your mind—not outside events. Realize this, and you will find strength," exhorts Marcus Aurelius in *Meditations*, as a reminder to focus on controlling his thinking and not let himself become reactive to external factors. This idea can be applied to contexts like work and personal relationships, where many outcomes are influenced by external factors not under your control.

Reflection and Mindfulness

The Stoics practiced daily reflection to develop self-awareness and ensure that their actions aligned with their values. Seneca recommends doing this nightly: "We should every night call ourselves to an account: What infirmity have I mastered today? What passions opposed? What temptation resisted? What virtue acquired?" Such reflections develop mindfulness while encouraging a focused and intentional approach to daily living.

Professional Development

By being mindful of your thoughts and emotions, you can look at situations objectively and respond appropriately. A manager might use Stoic principles to handle workplace conflicts calmly, focusing on constructive responses rather than reacting emotionally.

Personal Relationships

In personal relationships, Stoicism can help people foster healthier and more beneficial relations. By focusing on your own choices and behaviors, and recognizing that others are not under your control, you can be more accepting of differences and respond to conflicts with understanding rather than frustration.

Self-Improvement

For personal growth, Stoicism encourages cultivating self-discipline, reflecting on daily progress, and viewing hardships as keys to growth. As Seneca says, "A setback has often cleared the way for greater prosperity. Many things have fallen only to rise to more exalted heights." So, even when you fail at something, it may end up making you better off in the long run.

Contentment in Daily Life

With its focus on living a good life, Stoicism teaches people to be content in the present moment. By maintaining mindfulness in the present, you can decrease your anxiety and maintain your inner peace. As Seneca writes, "The happy man is satisfied with his present situation, no matter what it is, and eyes his fortune with contentment; the happy man is the one who permits reason to evaluate every condition of his existence."

Stoicism is more than just a philosophy; it's a practical tool kit for personal development and self-help. By teaching people to focus on what they can control, manage their emotions, and view life's challenges as opportunities, Stoicism provides timeless guidance that empowers people to lead more fulfilling lives. As Marcus Aurelius believed, the power to improve one's life lies within oneself, not in one's circumstances. This enduring message makes Stoicism an invaluable resource for anyone looking to enhance their personal and professional growth in today's fast-paced world.

STOICISM IN THE WORKPLACE AND LEADERSHIP

From the Senate to the Boardroom

Quotable Voices

"Never value anything as profitable that compels you to break your promise, to lose your self-respect, to hate any man, to suspect, to curse, to act the hypocrite, to desire anything that needs walls and curtains."

—Marcus Aurelius

Throughout history, Stoic principles and teachings have had a profound impact on leaders in politics and business. With its focus on ethical behavior, rational decision-making, and compassion and empathy in dealing with others, Stoicism offers a guide for modern leaders to navigate many challenges of leadership. It also helps with creating positive work environments and acts as a guide for how to conduct oneself with coworkers.

STOICISM IN THE WORKPLACE

Stoicism can be easily applied to the workplace within the following categories.

Emotional Regulation

In high-pressure environments, the Stoic practice of regulating and rationally dealing with emotions can be invaluable. Leaders can benefit from the Stoic techniques of maintaining composure, making clearheaded decisions, and responding calmly to crises.

Detachment and Compassion

Stoicism promotes emotional detachment, which might seem counterintuitive to compassionate governance. However, this detachment refers to not being overwhelmed by emotions, allowing leaders to make compassionate decisions that are not biased by personal feelings.

Ethical Leadership

"There is nothing dangerous in a man's having as much power as he likes if he takes the view that he has power to do only what it is his duty to do," writes Seneca. This quote suggests that it's not the position that corrupts but the person behind it. Stoicism places a strong emphasis on virtue and ethics, which can guide leadership practices. A Stoic leader prioritizes fairness, integrity, and the common good, making decisions that are not just profitable but also just and moral.

Vulnerability in Leadership

While Stoicism is often associated with emotional control, it also advocates for understanding and dealing with human emotions intelligently. A Stoic leader can show vulnerability by acknowledging their limitations and uncertainties, which enhances authenticity and relatability. In dealing with coworkers, an empathetic and compassionate leader would do well to follow the advice of Marcus Aurelius: "Accustom yourself not to be disregarding of what someone else has to say: as far as possible enter into the mind of the speaker."

Passion versus Indifference

While passion is typically seen as a driver in business success, Stoicism promotes an attitude of rational indifference to outcomes. This doesn't mean Stoicism promotes a lack of effort; this philosophy places focus on actions rather than being tied to a specific result, which can reduce undue stress. By focusing on what you can do, it may lead to more sustainable, steady, and reliable leadership in the face of challenges.

Employee Relationships
Stoic principles can guide leaders in managing relationships with empathy and respect, recognizing the value of each team member, and fostering a supportive and positive work environment. Epictetus offers advice on how to view positions of leadership: "If you have been placed in a position above others, are you automatically going to behave like a despot? Remember who you are and whom you govern—that they are kinsmen, brothers by nature, fellow descendants of Zeus." Basically, this means that you need to treat your employees as humans—that you're not any better than they are.

Resilience and Adaptability
Stoicism teaches resilience and the acceptance of things beyond one's control; these are crucial traits for navigating the uncertainties and rapid changes in today's complex world. For example, you can use the Stoic practice of negative visualization to plan for possible challenges, following the advice of Seneca: "It is in times of security that the spirit should be preparing itself for difficult times; while fortune is bestowing favors on it, then is the time for it to be strengthened against her rebuffs."

EXAMPLES OF STOIC LEADERSHIP

Consider the following examples of Stoic leadership in ancient and modern times.

Marcus Aurelius

The moral philosopher Lord John Acton noted that throughout history those with great power usually succumbed to abusing that power for personal gain. According to Acton, "Power tends to corrupt, and absolute power corrupts absolutely." Yet as emperor of the Roman Empire, Marcus Aurelius was the most powerful man in the world, and his dedication to maintaining his moral center helped him lead Rome through war, plague, and flood. His leadership exemplified Stoic ideals by focusing on his duties and responsibilities, seeking the common good, and maintaining inner peace amidst external chaos.

Modern Leaders

Many effective modern leaders, while not specifically attributing their leadership styles to Stoicism, have attributes that the Stoics advocated for. For example, Tim Cook, the CEO of Apple, is known for his thoughtful, methodical, and long-term approach to guiding his company. Cook's emphasis on privacy, environmental sustainability, and human rights aligns with Stoic values of doing what is right and just in the face of external pressures.

As CEO of Microsoft, Satya Nadella has been instrumental in transforming the company's culture. While in his role, Nadella has emphasized practicing empathy, learning from failures, and looking beyond the short term. His focus on personal growth and reflection resonates with Stoic practices of self-improvement and managing one's perceptions and reactions.

The challenges of modern leadership are complex and ever evolving. Leaders who ground themselves in the core principles of Stoicism can use its timeless principles to deal with accelerating changes brought on by technology, societal change, and economic turbulence.

OUR HUMAN CONTRACT

Stoics and Public Life

Quotable Voices

"The duty of a man is to be useful to his fellow-men; if possible, to be useful to many of them; failing this, to be useful to a few; failing this, to be useful to his neighbors, and, failing them, to himself: for when he helps others, he advances the general interests of mankind."

—Seneca

Throughout the ancient world, the Stoics advocated being active in public life. Marcus Aurelius was emperor, Seneca was a statesman and advisor to Nero, and other rulers sought the advice of Epictetus. Because of their focus on actively living a life of virtue and seeking the common good, Stoic principles have influenced governance, leadership, and civic engagement.

STOIC PRINCIPLES IN GOVERNANCE

The Stoics have specific principles regarding governance, like the following.

Service to the Community

Because of the belief that all humans are part of the grand tapestry of the *Logos*, Stoicism advocates for cosmopolitanism—the notion that all human beings belong to a single community, based on mutual respect and understanding. As Epictetus teaches, "Do as

Socrates did, never replying to the question of where he was from with, 'I am Athenian,' or 'I am from Corinth,' but always, 'I am a citizen of the world.'"

Marcus Aurelius writes in *Meditations*, "Labor willingly and diligently, undistracted and aware of the common interest." He felt that his position as emperor was one of service, which translated into public policies that promoted social justice and equality.

Role of Virtue

Stoicism teaches that virtue should be the guiding principle in both personal life and public affairs. According to Stoicism, leaders are expected to demonstrate virtues like wisdom, justice, courage, and temperance. Marcus Aurelius thought that rather than seeking personal gain or glory, one should always work toward the greater good, writing, "It is not right that anything of any other kind, such as praise from the many, or power, or enjoyment of pleasure, should come into competition with that which is rationally and politically and practically good."

Emotional Resilience in Leadership

Stoic principles emphasize the importance of leaders maintaining emotional resilience and composure, especially in crisis situations. Instead of blaming circumstances or other people for failures, Stoic leadership encourages taking responsibility and making rational, clearheaded decisions that are in everyone's best interest.

Acceptance and Proactivity

Stoicism teaches acceptance of things one cannot change, while also advocating for proactive engagement in areas one can influence. This balance is crucial in public policy, where some issues require acceptance of complex realities, while others demand active intervention.

For example, mental health challenges are a part of human experience that cannot be completely eradicated. Stoicism encourages acceptance of this reality, reducing the stigma and unrealistic expectations of a "perfect" mental state. Policymakers can proactively address mental health by funding services, promoting awareness, and integrating mental health into broader public health initiatives. By doing so, they improve the quality of life for those affected, even if the underlying challenges remain.

Living According to Nature

When the Stoics advocated living according to nature, they also understood that people need to work with others according to their natures. This means being understanding and compassionate toward those you disagree with (due to politics, background, etc.) and finding ways to work together for the common good. Marcus Aurelius reminded himself to be gracious toward difficult people, advocating, "When you wake up in the morning, tell yourself: The people I deal with today will be meddling, ungrateful, arrogant, dishonest, jealous, and surly. They are like this because they can't tell good from evil."

EXAMPLES OF STOICS IN PUBLIC LIFE

Here are some examples of Stoicism in public life.

Cato the Younger

A Roman statesman known for his unwavering Stoic integrity, Cato the Younger had a leadership style defined by his staunch opposition to Julius Caesar. His commitment to the Roman Republic's principles and his refusal to compromise on his beliefs—even to the death—made him a symbol of virtue and republican liberty. His life exemplifies the Stoic ideal of living and dying according to one's principles, regardless of the external costs.

Thomas Jefferson

Thomas Jefferson, one of the founding fathers of the United States, was deeply influenced by the writings of the Stoics. Jefferson often quoted Stoic philosophers in his letters, showing deep respect for their teachings on ethics and personal discipline. For instance, in a letter to William Short, he wrote, "Epictetus and Epicurus give us laws for governing ourselves," and he later wrote of his desire to write his own translation of the works of Epictetus as he found none of the existing translations tolerable. He saw Stoic philosophy as a guide for personal conduct, emphasizing virtue, self-control, and rational thought.

Modern Politicians and Stoicism

Other examples of excellent political leadership can be seen in the steadfast, calm, and compassionate leadership of Chancellor Angela Merkel of Germany and Prime Minister Jacinda Ardern of New Zealand. Both leaders helped usher their nations through the COVID-19 pandemic crisis, exhibiting rationality by basing their decisions on the latest science, communicating honestly and clearly, and leading by example. They stand in clear contrast with other leaders who tried to downplay the severity of the crisis or flaunted their mandated guidelines.

With justice as one of the four cardinal virtues of Stoicism, the Stoics believed that how a person treats other people is essential. They held that, rather than seeking power for personal gain, leadership and public service were avenues to make the world a better place for as many people as possible, regardless of who they are.

STOICISM AND RELATIONSHIPS

Navigating Interpersonal Connections Through
Ancient Wisdom

Quotable Voices
"But when you are looking on anyone as a friend when you do not
trust him as you trust yourself, you are making a grave mistake,
and have failed to grasp sufficiently the full force of true friendship."

—Seneca

Maintaining healthy and harmonious relationships can be a challenging part of life. Due to different personality types, cultures, and belief systems, there is no "one size fits all" solution to dealing with other people. Stoic philosophy, with its focus on self-control, rationality, and perspective, offers valuable insights into managing your interactions with others more effectively.

STOIC PERSPECTIVE ON RELATIONSHIPS

Stoics have many thoughts on relationships and how to navigate them, like the following.

The Social Nature of Humans

The Stoics posited that humans are social creatures and that relationships are a key part of human existence. Marcus Aurelius observes the importance of building strong and nurturing relationships:

"But he who values a rational soul, a soul universal and fitted for political life, regards nothing else except this; and above all things he keeps his soul in a condition and in an activity conformable to reason and social life, and he cooperates to this end with those who are of the same kind as himself."

—Marcus Aurelius

Justice

How humans interacted with each other was so important to the Stoics that they included justice as one of their four cardinal virtues. Justice is not just about laws, but how you treat other people. Because the Stoics held that people are all part of the same cosmic community, they taught that one should be patient with fellow humans. "[Treat] unenlightened souls with sympathy and indulgence," Epictetus explains, "Remembering that they are ignorant or mistaken about what's most important. Never be harsh, remember Plato's dictum: 'Every soul is deprived of the truth against its will.'"

Acceptance of Others

Marcus Aurelius reminded himself, "Accept things to which fate binds you, and love the people with whom fate brings you together, but do so with all your heart." While you may be able to choose your friends, you do not have a choice of the family you are born into, nor can you necessarily choose your coworkers or others that you deal with on a daily basis. Stoicism encourages people to accept others as they are, without trying to change them.

Self-Control

Stoicism teaches that a person's reactions to external events, not the events themselves, determine their emotional state. This principle is especially important in relationships, where emotions can run high. By focusing on your own responses and maintaining a composed demeanor, you can foster more stable relationships. As Epictetus teaches, "There is only one way to happiness and that is to cease worrying about things which are beyond the power of our will."

PRACTICAL STOIC ADVICE ON RELATIONSHIPS

Stoics have practical advice on relationships, such as the following.

Understanding Different Perspectives

"Acquire the habit of attending carefully to what is being said by another, and of entering, so far as possible, into the mind of the speaker," advises Marcus Aurelius as a reminder to listen to others with intention to try and understand their point of view. Stoicism encourages people to consider others' perspectives and motives without quick judgments. This empathetic approach can lead to deeper understanding and less conflict.

On Criticizing Others

Marcus Aurelius notes, "Whenever you are about to find fault with someone, ask yourself the following question: What fault of mine most nearly resembles the one I am about to criticize?" Keeping in mind that everyone has shortcomings can help you be more compassionate and understanding toward the faults of others.

Conflict Resolution

Using Stoic principles, people can approach conflicts calmly and constructively, focusing on solutions rather than blaming others or having an emotional reaction. This can lead to more productive discussions and less resentment. Seneca advises, "Nothing is burdensome if taken lightly, and nothing need arouse one's irritation so long as one doesn't make it bigger than it is by getting irritated." By not allowing what others say to irritate you, you are more likely to listen to what others say without reacting negatively, leading to better outcomes.

Kindness

The Stoics taught that people shouldn't just look out for their own well-being; they should also find ways to improve the lives of those around them. "One thing alone can bring us peace, an agreement to treat one another with kindness," penned Seneca, as a reminder that a person always has the choice to be kind to others in any situation.

Maintaining Personal Integrity

Since the actions of others are outside of one's control, the Stoics advocated that a person should focus on behaving with integrity and virtue regardless of how others behave. "It's silly to try to escape other people's faults. They are inescapable. Just try to escape your own," advises Marcus Aurelius. By focusing on personal virtues and self-improvement, you can bring your best self to your relationships, which is beneficial for all involved.

Stoicism offers a robust framework for improving and sustaining relationships. By adopting Stoic practices—focusing on your reactions, understanding others, and maintaining ethical conduct—you can build stronger, more resilient connections. In essence, Stoicism teaches that the quality of one's relationships depends not solely on the behavior of others but significantly on one's own responses and virtues. Their teachings can provide a practical guide for enhancing interpersonal dynamics that are applicable in modern times. In the words of Marcus Aurelius:

"Whenever you want to cheer yourself up, consider the good qualities of your companions, for example, the energy of one, the modesty of another, the generosity of yet another, and some other quality of another; for nothing cheers the heart as much as the images of excellence reflected in the character of our companions, all brought before us as fully as possible."

—Marcus Aurelius

THE UNIVERSE IS CHANGE

Stoicism for Coping with Change and Uncertainty

Quotable Voices

"Constantly bear in mind how many of these changes thou hast already witnessed. The universe is transformation: life is opinion."
—Marcus Aurelius

Throughout human history, there have been crises and challenges. From wars, famine, plagues, and earthquakes, to personal tragedy and struggles, humans have never been free of suffering. Sometimes change is something that you seek out, and other times change is forced upon you. Stoicism can be utilized to cope with change and uncertainty and offers a valuable perspective on managing life's inevitable challenges through a philosophical lens.

STOIC PRINCIPLES FOR DEALING WITH CHANGE

The Stoics had many concepts that dealt with change, like the following.

Dichotomy of Control

A central tenet of Stoicism is to understand that not all parts of life are controllable, and to accept that. By accepting that life is in a state of change, a person can adopt a mindset where change is seen as a normal part of life rather than something that disrupts how life "should be." This distinction is crucial in times of change and uncertainty, as it can help people to concentrate their energy and effort where it can actually make a difference. Epictetus taught his students, "If we try to adapt our mind to the regular sequence of changes and accept the inevitable with good grace, our life will proceed quite smoothly and harmoniously."

Preparation for Adversity

Stoics practiced premeditation of future hardships (*Premeditatio Malorum*), which helps in mentally preparing for the worst-case scenarios, reducing anxiety about the unknown, and making oneself more resilient when challenges do occur. As Seneca succinctly writes, "So I look for the best and am prepared for the opposite."

Value Neutrality

Much of one's distress about the challenges of life comes from one's perspective of the obstacles in one's way. Stoicism teaches that external changes and events are not inherently good or bad; one's judgments about them make them so. Marcus Aurelius says, "Things stand outside of us, themselves by themselves, neither knowing anything of themselves nor expressing any judgment. What is it, then, that passes judgment on them? The ruling faculty." By reassessing your perceptions of change and uncertainty, and viewing them as a natural part of life, you can face them with courage and maintain inner tranquility.

Virtue As Sufficient for Happiness

Stoicism posits that living virtuously, in accordance with reason and ethical principles, is sufficient for happiness. By focusing on living according to virtue regardless of what circumstances a person finds themself in, they have a guide for how to approach any challenges. This idea can be particularly empowering in times of uncertainty, suggesting that despite external circumstances, a person's character and choices can sustain well-being.

Embracing Rather Than Avoiding Uncertainty

The Stoics understood that a person could never live a life without challenges or adversity. Contrary to the natural desire to seek stability and avoid uncertainty, Stoics found value in embracing the unpredictable as a means to practice and strengthen virtue. By viewing obstacles as opportunities to strengthen your character and abilities, this approach transforms challenges into opportunities for personal growth.

Negative Emotions As Useful

While Stoicism advocates controlling irrational and harmful emotions, it also acknowledges the usefulness of some negative emotions when experienced rationally. For instance, rational fear can prompt caution and preventive actions without leading to panic or despair.

Indifference to Pleasure

In a culture that often pursues pleasure as a primary goal, Stoicism's view of pleasure as an "indifferent" (neither good nor bad) is counterintuitive. The Stoics understood that pleasure and suffering were transitory, and therefore rather than seeking pleasure, Stoics focused on how one enjoys pleasures or endures suffering, emphasizing moderation and self-control. As Marcus Aurelius notes, "Remember, too, on every occasion that leads you to vexation to apply this principle: not that this is a misfortune, but that to bear it nobly is good fortune."

EXAMPLES OF APPLYING STOIC PRINCIPLES

The following are some examples of applying Stoic principles to handle uncertainty and change in life.

Stock Market Volatility

Investors who apply Stoic principles focus on their strategies and decisions rather than market fluctuations, accepting losses as part of the process and enjoying gains without becoming overly attached. While not a Stoic in the traditional sense, Warren Buffett's approach to investing is very Stoic: "To be fearful when others are greedy and to be greedy only when others are fearful." His practice of maintaining a clear perspective highlights his rational, disciplined strategy to investing, which resonates with Stoic principles of not following the crowd and maintaining emotional control in decision-making.

Career Changes

When faced with an unexpected job loss, you can use Stoic teachings to maintain composure, seeing it as an opportunity to explore new paths and grow rather than as a setback. Seneca advises: "So you have to get used to your circumstances, complain about them as little as possible, and grasp whatever advantage they have to offer: no condition is so bitter that a stable mind cannot find some consolation in it."

Public Leaders in Crisis

When faced with a crisis, leaders would do well to adopt Stoic qualities to reduce panic and rally support for more effective handling of challenges. For example, Winston Churchill led the United Kingdom through World War II with a calm and determined demeanor, exhibiting Stoic qualities while focusing on actionable steps and maintaining hope and morale.

Life rarely ever goes to plan, and your perspective is key to facing challenges and disruptions. Stoicism provides practical tools and philosophical insights for dealing with change and uncertainty, making it a valuable resource for individuals seeking to cultivate resilience, make reasoned decisions, and maintain inner peace in a turbulent world.

CARE FOR THE BODY

A Tool for Virtue

Quotable Voices

"Health is the soul that animates all the enjoyments of life,
which fade and are tasteless without it."

—Seneca

Stoicism, while typically associated with mental and emotional discipline, also relates to physical well-being. Because your body is the vehicle through which you experience the world, taking care of your physical health should also be of paramount importance. How you feel physically impacts your mood and mental outlook, therefore maintaining your physical health helps to improve your mental health.

STOIC PRINCIPLES REGARDING PHYSICAL HEALTH

Stoics have many principles that pertain to one's physical body, like the following.

The Body As a Tool for Virtue

Stoics viewed the body primarily as an instrument for practicing virtue. It should be kept in good health so a person can do their duty and live according to virtue. In an age where health and fitness can sometimes lead to extreme diets and workout routines, Stoicism suggests a minimalist approach—sufficient for maintaining health but not obsessive, aligning with the natural needs of the body rather than societal or aesthetic expectations.

Seneca teaches, "Hold fast, then, to this sound and wholesome rule of life—that you indulge the body only so far as is needful for good health. The body should be treated more rigorously, that it may not be disobedient to the mind," advocating for moderation of physical exercise and diet. Excess is seen as contrary to rational living, and maintaining physical health should not be driven by vanity but by the desire to remain functionally fit.

Indifference to Pain and Comfort

Stoics taught that physical sensations, whether pain or pleasure, should not disturb the rational mind. By practicing control over the body, a Stoic is better able to control their responses to external stimuli. As Epictetus teaches, "Faced with pain, you will discover the power of endurance. If you are insulted, you will discover patience. In time, you will grow to be confident that there is not a single impression that you will not have the moral means to tolerate," recommending that one develop resilience and a balanced approach to physical experiences.

Connection Between Mind and Body

Marcus Tullius Cicero, a Roman statesman and philosopher who often wrote about Stoic philosophy, writes, "In a disordered mind, as in a disordered body, soundness of health is impossible." While Stoicism emphasizes the supremacy of the mind, it also acknowledges the interdependence between mental and physical health. A neglected body can impair the mind, and vice versa.

Welcoming Discomfort

Musonius Rufus advocated voluntary discomfort to practice control over the body and physical appetites: "We will train both soul and body when we accustom ourselves to cold, heat, thirst, hunger, scarcity of food, hardness of bed, abstaining from pleasures, and enduring pains." The body and soul are tested in a variety of different physical states (from hunger to where you sleep), all of which can be helpful.

Fasting and Restraint

As Seneca observes, "Pleasures, when they go beyond a certain limit, are but punishments." Practices like fasting and eating simple food are seen as ways to strengthen the will and detach from physical dependencies. Seneca even recommends fasting to practice self-discipline, stating, "A stomach firmly under control, one that will put up with hard usage, marks a considerable step toward independence." Learning to control your physical desires can become a philosophical practice to prepare for hardships in life.

Alcohol

Because of the Stoics' emphasis on moderation and maintaining self-control, tempering the use of alcohol was considered important to living a life of virtue. As Seneca points out, "Drunkenness inflames and lays bare every vice, removing the reserve that acts as a chuck on impulses to wrong behavior." Excessive use of alcohol also brings on several health issues, limiting a person's abilities and usefulness in contributing to the greater community.

Emotional Indifference to Health Issues

Stoics strove to remain emotionally indifferent to health outcomes. While they valued the effort put into maintaining health, they accepted that illness or physical decline may happen regardless of these efforts. Marcus Aurelius, who suffered from various physical ailments throughout his life, writes, "He who is afraid of pain will sometimes also be afraid of some of the things that will happen in the world, and even this is impiety." Practicing this kind of detachment helps maintain tranquility, even in suffering.

Diet and Simplicity

Seneca wrote often about the importance of living a simple life, including diet:

"Cling, therefore, to this sound and wholesome plan of life; indulge the body just so far as suffices for good health. . . . Your food should appease your hunger, your drink quench your thirst, your clothing keep out the cold, your house be a protection against inclement weather. It makes no difference whether it is built of turf or variegated marble imported from another country."

—Seneca

Musonius Rufus advocated for a vegetarian diet, primarily for its simplicity and naturalness. He writes, "Just as plants receive nourishment for survival, not pleasure—for humans, food is the medicine of life." Rufus's words place significant emphasis on simple living, which included eating only what was necessary for survival and maintaining health.

Rest and Rejuvenation

As part of the Stoic virtue of moderation, Seneca urged that everyone needs rest to remain more mentally aware. "Just as you must not force fertile farmland, as uninterrupted productivity will soon exhaust it, so constant effort will sap our mental vigor, while a short period of rest and relaxation will restore our powers." He also recommended that one take time to enjoy nature, writing, "We must go for walks out of doors, so that the mind can be strengthened by a clear sky and plenty of fresh air."

While the Stoics clearly focused on control over the mind, they understood the body was the vessel of the human experience and therefore needed to be taken care of through disciplined diet, physical exercise, voluntary discomfort, and rest. Stoicism provides a rational framework for approaching physical health, emphasizing a balanced lifestyle that supports both mental and physical well-being, without succumbing to the extremes often seen in contemporary health cultures.

STOICISM AND THE ROLE OF PHYSICAL EXERCISE AND DISCIPLINE

Mind over Matter

Quotable Voices

"For obviously the philosopher's body should be well prepared
for physical activity, because often the virtues make use of this
as a necessary instrument for the affairs of life."

—Musonius Rufus

While the Stoics placed mental fitness as the primary focus of their philosophy, physical fitness and discipline were also an important part of the development of the self. The Stoics saw strengthening the body as a practice to help strengthen the mind, and as key to living a virtuous life.

STOIC PRINCIPLES FOR PHYSICAL ENDURANCE

Stoics have several principles for physical endurance too, including the following.

Discipline

"If you are careless and lazy now and keep putting things off and always deferring the day after which you will attend to yourself, you will not notice that you are making no progress but you will live and die as someone quite ordinary," teaches Epictetus, advocating that individuals practice discipline in all aspects of life. Stoics believed physical exercise was important not merely to improve bodily health but also to develop self-control and mental fortitude. Cato the Younger, known for his physical endurance, states, "Flee laziness, because the indolence of the soul is the decay of the body."

Reaching Your Potential

The Stoics advocated the holistic development of human beings and believed that a person should strengthen the mind and the body to reach their highest potential. They may have taken their cue from Socrates, who was well known for his endurance and had served with distinction in the military, and who once said, "No man has the right to be an amateur in the matter of physical training. It is a shame for a man to grow old without seeing the beauty and strength of which his body is capable."

Exercise As a Form of Preparation

Following the Stoic principle of preparing for adversity (*Premeditatio Malorum*), physical exercise prepares the body and mind for hardships. It's about strengthening oneself against future physical and psychological challenges. This is why the Stoics recommend that a person choose to undergo discomforts of their own choosing so that they are prepared for when discomforts come unexpectedly.

Practicing Restraint and Welcoming Hardship

Musonius Rufus, one of the lesser-known Stoic philosophers, observed that a comfortable and easy life can lead to poor health, and that hardship and restraint, whether by choice or forced, can improve one's physical well-being: "Others have been in poor health from overindulgence and high living, before exile has provided strength, forcing them to live a more vigorous life."

Exercise for Virtue, Not Pleasure

Unlike modern views that often link exercise to aesthetic goals or pleasure, Stoics focused on exercising for the sake of virtue. Exercise should serve the purpose of maintaining health and enabling effective action, not for vanity or extreme feats of strength. As Marcus Aurelius explains, "The body ought to be compact, and to show no irregularity either in motion or attitude. For what the mind shows in the face by maintaining in it the expression of intelligence and propriety, that ought to be required also in the whole body. But all of these things should be observed without affectation."

Resilience Through Voluntary Discomfort

Stoics often practiced voluntary discomfort—such as cold showers or fasting—to enhance their mental resilience. This extended to exercise, where the challenge is embraced not just for physical benefits but for strengthening the will and character as well. Physical discipline was also seen as a reflection of inner discipline and consistency.

Indifference to Pain

Stoicism teaches indifference to pain and physical discomfort, viewing them as opportunities to practice endurance and detachment. This can lead to a more mindful and less reactive approach to physical challenges. Marcus Aurelius writes that enduring pain should not keep a person from acting rationally, and that one needs to keep pain in perspective:

"Whenever you suffer pain, keep in mind that it's nothing to be ashamed of and that it can't degrade your guiding intelligence, nor keep it from acting rationally and for the common good. And in most cases you should be helped by the saying of Epicurus, that pain is never unbearable or unending, so you can remember these limits and not add to them in your imagination. Remember too that many common annoyances are pain in disguise, such as sleepiness, fever, and loss of appetite. When they start to get you down, tell yourself you are giving in to pain."

—Marcus Aurelius

Welcoming Failure in Exercise

The Stoics often used examples of physical activities to illustrate their principles. Epictetus once said, "The true man is revealed in difficult times. So when trouble comes, think of yourself as a wrestler whom God, like a trainer, has paired with a tough young buck. For what purpose? To turn you into Olympic-class material. But this is going to take some sweat to accomplish." In Stoic practice, failure during physical training (such as not completing a set number of reps or a run) is seen not as a negative but as a chance to practice acceptance, to reflect on physical limits, and to work on self-improvement.

Examples of Stoic Endurance

The Stoics themselves were excellent examples of practicing physical endurance. Cleanthes, who took over the Stoic school after Zeno, did backbreaking work as a water carrier at night to support himself. Chrysippus, who led the Stoic school after Cleanthes, trained as a long-distance runner. Marcus Aurelius himself enthusiastically trained in wrestling in his youth. Each understood the importance of training the body as well as the mind.

Modern Application

You can see in modern militaries that the development of physical endurance is not just about being able to fight. For instance, the Navy SEALs' "Hell Week" is not just about physical toughness but also about cultivating mental resilience, aligning closely with Stoic practices.

While Stoicism focuses heavily on the development of the mind, it enriches the understanding of physical exercise, framing it as a crucial element in the pursuit of a disciplined, virtuous life and concentrating on long-term health and resilience, rather than considering it as merely a tool for achieving physical attractiveness or temporary pleasures.

SELF-ACCEPTANCE

Stoicism and Self-Esteem

Quotable Voices
"The wise man is neither raised up by prosperity nor cast down by adversity; for always he has striven to rely predominantly on himself, and to derive all joy from himself."

—Seneca

Following Stoicism, you can focus on rationally observing your thoughts and emotions to foster a healthier relationship with yourself by developing an objective outlook about your shortcomings. Since you are in control of your opinions about yourself, you have the power to change those opinions by using Stoic principles. Rather than berating yourself for your deficiencies, you can take an objective appraisal of your flaws so that you can improve.

UNDERSTANDING WHAT IS WITHIN YOUR CONTROL

Central to Stoic philosophy is the distinction between what you can and cannot control. Self-acceptance in Stoicism involves recognizing and accepting your limitations, while focusing on improving aspects of your character within your control. Epictetus teaches that a wise person recognizes that they control their emotional well-being: "The mark and attitude of the ordinary man: never look for help or harm from yourself, only from outsiders. The mark and attitude of the philosopher: look for help and harm exclusively from yourself."

Virtue As the Basis of Self-Worth

The Stoics believed that virtue—wisdom, courage, justice, and temperance—is the sole true good and should be the basis of self-esteem. A person's happiness is internal, not driven by external forces. This contrasts with modern views that often base self-worth on achievements, status, or emotional states. By focusing your efforts on improving your virtue with moral consistency and integrity, you can abide by your principles and be a good person in any situation.

Emotional Resilience and Self-Compassion

Seneca writes, "What progress, you ask, have I made? I have begun to be a friend to myself." Stoicism teaches the management of emotions through reason, which fosters resilience. Part of that rationality includes approaching yourself with compassion rather than harsh self-criticism, understanding human imperfections, and striving for improvement without self-loathing. Seneca cautions against dwelling on past mistakes, writing, "What is the point of dragging up sufferings that are over, of being miserable now, because you were miserable then?"

The Role of Reflection and Self-Awareness

Marcus Aurelius writes, "For nowhere either with more quiet or more freedom from trouble does a man retire than into his own soul, particularly when he has within him such thoughts that by looking into them he is immediately in perfect tranquility." Often, negative emotions are caused by one's misjudgments of things, including the emotions, themselves. By practicing self-reflection and becoming more aware of your thoughts, you can change your opinions about your circumstances and about yourself to better align with Stoic virtues and principles.

Indifference to External Validation

Stoicism teaches indifference to external opinions and conditions, focusing instead on internal virtues. Self-acceptance comes from aligning with your rational judgments and ethical standards, rather than seeking external validation. Marcus Aurelius writes in *Meditations*, "It never ceases to amaze me: we all love ourselves more than other people, but care more about their opinion than our own." This teaches that the view that you take of yourself is far more important than the opinions others have of you.

The Stoics also taught that a person's reputation is something that is not under their control, meaning that you have no control over what others think or say about you, and you should therefore not be disturbed by rumors. Epictetus explains that people often judge others not from a place of malice but from their own misperceptions:

"When any person harms you, or speaks badly of you, remember that he acts or speaks from a supposition of its being his duty. Now, it is not possible that he should follow what appears right to you, but what appears so to himself. Therefore, if he judges from a wrong appearance, he is the person hurt, since he too is the person deceived."

—Epictetus

When you keep this in mind you can also be more compassionate toward others because you recognize that they are making judgments from their own perception of things, not yours.

Welcoming Discomfort

Emotionally uncomfortable situations are seen as opportunities to grow and strengthen one's character in Stoicism. Rather than turning away from emotionally challenging situations, you can embrace your personal flaws and mistakes as chances to learn and apply Stoic virtues.

Rational Control over Emotions

The idea that you can, and *should*, control your emotional responses through reason is somewhat counterintuitive in a culture that often encourages expressing and valuing emotions as they are. Stoics argued that rational evaluation of emotions can lead to greater emotional health and, subsequently, deeper self-acceptance.

Comparison to Others

The Stoics recognized that much discontentment within a person comes from comparing oneself to others. Someone may feel like they are a lesser person because they are not attractive, wealthy, or famous. But the Stoics understood that these things are external and thus are not important to their internal happiness.

In talking about wealth, Seneca writes, "I shall borrow from Epicurus: 'The acquisition of riches has been for many men, not an end, but a change, of troubles.' I do not wonder. For the fault is not in the wealth, but in the mind itself." This teaching suggests that how a person thinks about external things can cause discontentment, while learning to think with gratitude can lead to contentment.

Stoicism provides a robust framework for achieving self-acceptance through rational self-assessment, emotional resilience, and alignment with internal virtues rather than external standards. By looking inward with compassion, you can follow the advice of Marcus Aurelius: "Dig within. Within is the wellspring of good; and it is always ready to bubble up, if you just dig."

COMPARISON WITH OTHERS

The Thief of Joy

Quotable Voices

"Let us take pleasure in what we have received and make no comparison; no man will ever be happy if tortured by the greater happiness of another."

—Seneca

Much of the unhappiness of life comes from comparing oneself to others, ultimately creating feelings of deficiency and failure. The Stoics taught that this comparison was a focus on external things and, therefore, should be treated indifferently. Stoic principles can help you focus on your personal development without worrying about the success or opinions of others.

STOIC IDEAS ABOUT COMPARISON

Stoics had many ideas about comparison, like the following.

Self-Referential Improvement

Stoicism teaches that a person can't control others' actions, behaviors, or successes; they can only control their own reactions and their own self-improvement. Adopting an introspective focus helps cultivate your personal virtues, leading to better results than if you were to compete with external standards that are outside your control.

Controlling Desires

The Stoics taught that by reducing one's desires, a person can find contentment with what they have, rather than feeling the lack of what they don't. Seneca cautions about the value of sought-after things:

"So, concerning the things we pursue, and for which we vigorously exert ourselves, we owe this consideration—either there is nothing useful in them, or most aren't useful. Some of them are superfluous, while others aren't worth that much. But we don't discern this and see them as free, when they cost us dearly."

—Seneca

In other words, sometimes what you pursue is simply not worthwhile—in fact, these things may harm you in some way.

The Role of Envy and Jealousy

Stoics observed that negative emotions (like envy) arise from comparisons. They suggest ways to overcome those emotions through rational thinking and focusing on personal virtues. Marcus Aurelius notes, "How much time he gains who does not look to see what his neighbor says or does or thinks, but only at what he does himself, to make it just and holy."

The Role of Fate

Because of the Stoics' belief in fate, these philosophers believed that things often don't work out as desired because of external, uncontrollable events and circumstances. By recognizing that outcomes are never certain, you can focus on your choices and actions, not the outcome. Seneca muses about the fickleness of fate: "Never have I put my trust in fortune, even when she appeared to be offering peace; all those gifts she bestowed on me in her kindness—position, influence—I stored where she would be able to reclaim them with no disturbance to me."

Value of Individual Paths

Stoicism respects the uniqueness of everyone's path and challenges the idea that success or value is relative to others' situations or achievements. You can work on your own virtue and take actions that align with your principles, leading to inner peace regardless of external success or failures. As Seneca writes:

"So what you need is not those more radical remedies which we have now finished with—blocking yourself here, being angry with yourself there, threatening yourself sternly somewhere else—but the final treatment, confidence in yourself and the belief that you are on the right path, and not led astray by the many tracks which cross yours of people who are hopelessly lost, though some are wandering not far from the true path."

—Seneca

Comparison As a Tool for Motivation

While generally advising against comparisons, the Stoics advised looking to those with admirable traits and doing one's best to emulate those traits. As Seneca advised Lucilius,

> "Choose [someone] whose life, conversation, and soul-expressing face have satisfied you; picture him always to yourself as your protector or your pattern. For we must indeed have someone according to whom we may regulate our characters; you can never straighten that which is crooked unless you use a ruler."
>
> —Seneca

Essentially, observing others can serve as a motivational tool and inspire self-improvement, if used rationally.

Accepting Your Limitations

Contrary to modern society that often praises excelling in all areas, Stoicism suggests living a life of virtue, focusing on one's strengths, and accepting one's limitations. Epictetus, advising on how to approach one's career, gave the question and answer, "'Well, what will my profession in the community be?' Whatever position you are equipped to fill, so long as you preserve the man of trust and integrity."

Indifference to Praise and Criticism

Stoicism teaches indifference to both praise and criticism, which is counterintuitive in a culture that often seeks validation. This teaching is important in a modern culture dominated by social media where comparison with others is rampant because the opinions of others are outside of your control. A Stoic understands that true contentment comes from knowing they are living a virtuous life, not from external validation.

Comparison and Historical Figures

Stoics like Cato the Younger remained focused on their own principles and living according to virtue. Cato faced political and personal setbacks, yet he did not succumb to despair even when others prospered through what he saw as dishonorable means. He was considered a paragon of virtue but cared little for praise and honor, stating, "I would much rather have men ask why I have no statue than why I have one."

Contemporary Stoic Practitioners

Modern examples of successful Stoics include athletes such as Dutch speed skater Mark Tuitert. Because he believed that he had to work harder than his competition, he followed a rigorous and exhausting workout regimen. After failing twice to qualify for the Olympics due to overtraining, he credits Stoicism with helping him to find balance and stay mentally focused—regardless of the actions of his competitors—and won a gold medal in the 1500 meter speed skating at the 2010 Winter Olympics.

Stoicism offers valuable insights into dealing with comparison, fostering a healthier self-relation, and promoting a life focused on personal virtues rather than external validation. By adopting its practical strategies, you can better navigate a world where comparison is often unavoidable.

HOW TO DEAL WITH ENEMIES

Benevolence over Retaliation

Quotable Voices

"We ought always to deal justly, not only with those who are just to us, but likewise to those who endeavor to injure us; and this, for fear lest by rendering them evil for evil, we should fall into the same vice."

—Hierocles

Conflict with others is something that humans have dealt with throughout existence. However, Stoicism can offer unique insight into managing conflict and interpersonal challenges with composure and wisdom. By changing your perspective toward others who disagree or work against you, you can defuse situations and work toward more amiable resolutions.

STOIC PRINCIPLES AND CONFLICT

Stoics espoused many principles relating to conflict, including the following.

Control over Reactions

A central tenet in Stoicism is managing what you can control—your thoughts and reactions. When dealing with enemies, Stoics focused on maintaining their own virtue and composure, rather than trying to control the other person. Epictetus teaches that it is a person's perspective on something that causes them harm:

"Remember, it is not enough to be hit or insulted to be harmed, you must believe that you are being harmed. If someone succeeds in provoking you, realize that your mind is complicit in the provocation. [. . .] Take a moment before reacting, and you will find it is easier to maintain control."

—Epictetus

No True Enemies

Stoicism teaches that external events, including the actions of others, are not inherently good or bad but something that allows an individual to practice virtue. The labeling of someone as an enemy is based on your perception and judgment. "I have seen the beauty of good, and the ugliness of evil," writes Marcus Aurelius. "And have recognized that the wrongdoer has a nature related to my own—not of the same blood or birth, but the same mind, and possessing a share of the divine." Here, Marcus Aurelius speaks about the interconnectedness of all humans and showing kindness even to those that did him wrong.

Compassion and Understanding

Stoicism also asserts that people act according to their understanding of good. Additionally, those who oppose or harm others are not enemies in the traditional sense but are misguided in their perceptions. As Epictetus explains, "[When someone does something you don't like] Say to yourself each time, 'He did what he believed was right.'" Stoicism encourages understanding that those who wrong you are often acting out of ignorance of what's good and evil. Thus, a Stoic strives to respond with empathy and pity rather than with hostility.

Benevolence over Retaliation

It may seem counterintuitive to respond to hostility with kindness; however, Stoicism would advocate benevolence over retaliation, promoting peace over continued conflict. Seneca advises, "How much better to heal than seek revenge from injury. Vengeance wastes a lot of time and exposes you to many more injuries than the first that sparked it. Anger always outlasts hurt. Best to take the opposite course." This quotation explains that a person should act rationally and with kindness toward those who they feel have wronged them, as negative emotions cause more harm to them.

Indifference to Harm

The Stoics practiced emotional detachment from harm done by others, viewing their own inner virtue as more important than external actions. This can lead to a surprising lack of animosity toward those who might be considered enemies. Marcus Aurelius explains how to adopt this perspective: "Take away your opinion, and then there is taken away the complaint, 'I have been harmed.' Take away the complaint, 'I have been harmed,' and the harm is taken away."

Epictetus, known for using colorful anecdotes to illustrate Stoic principles, gives a great example of dealing with conflict while keeping calm: "Once, when [Agrippinus] was preparing for lunch, a messenger arrived from Rome announcing that Nero had sentenced him to exile. Unflustered, he replied, 'Then why don't we just move our lunch to Aricia.'" Rather than becoming upset or seeking revenge at the capricious nature of Emperor Nero, Agrippinus accepted his fate graciously.

Learning from Your Enemies

Stoics saw adversity, including dealing with enemies, as an opportunity to practice virtues such as patience, resilience, and forgiveness. Marcus Aurelius writes, "The best way of avenging yourself is not to become like the wrongdoer." You can take this as a reminder to not let those who wrong you change your behavior and to maintain your integrity even in the face of conflict.

STOIC EXAMPLES

Following are some examples of Stoics relating to conflict.

Marcus Aurelius

Despite being an emperor engaged in numerous military campaigns, Marcus Aurelius often wrote about dealing with opposition and betrayal with a philosophical and measured approach. Rather than punishing those who opposed him harshly, he sought to understand and forgive. He constantly questioned himself in his *Meditations*, such as asking, "With what are you discontented? With the badness of men? Recall to your mind this conclusion, that rational animals exist for one another, and that to endure is a part of justice, and that men do wrong involuntarily."

Bishop Desmond Tutu

"If you want peace, you don't talk to your friends. You talk to your enemies," said Desmond Tutu, who campaigned against apartheid in South Africa. He understood that the only way to move forward was through dialogue with those he disagreed with, and to make friends with his enemies. He often invited his opponents to talk to help find ways to work together, rather than seeking conflict.

Human relationships are complex and often difficult, and it can be challenging to find common ground with those who hold different opinions and values. Stoicism offers practical and philosophical guidance for dealing with enemies with its emphasis on rationality, control over emotions, and the transformative power of virtue in resolving conflicts.

REPUTATION

Why Should You Care What Others Think?

Quotable Voices

"I have often wondered how it is that every man loves himself
more than all the rest of men, but yet sets less value on his own
opinion of himself than on the opinion of others."

—Marcus Aurelius

Reputation is something that people tend to be concerned with. The
Stoic perspective regarding reputation and the (lack of) importance
of what others think presents a great opportunity to explore Stoic values. Stoics valued internal virtues but cast aside external judgments.

STOIC PERSPECTIVE ON REPUTATION

Stoics offered a unique perspective on reputation that in some ways
is in stark contrast with modern views.

Reputation Is Not under Your Control

In teaching about what is under one's control and what is not,
Epictetus clearly delineates on which side one's reputation falls:
"Some things are within our power, while others are not. Within
our power are opinion, motivation, desire, aversion, and, in a word,
whatever is of our own doing; not within our power are our body, our
property, reputation, office, and, in a word, whatever is not of our own
doing." While this is often a difficult thing to accept, what others
think of you is not under your control.

Opinions of Others

The Stoics understood that even if they do what they believe is the right thing, others will still find fault or disagree with the actions because everyone has different opinions. Epictetus recommends, "Whenever anyone criticizes or wrongs you, remember that they are only doing or saying what they think is right. They cannot be guided by your views, only their own."

This concept is important especially when it comes to social media, where comparison with others and the status of your reputation feels so important. As Epictetus teaches, "I laugh at those who think they can damage me. They do not know who I am, they do not know what I think, they cannot even touch the things which are really mine and with which I live." By recognizing that virtue is more important than what others think of you, you can keep your inner peace in the face of criticism or disparaging remarks.

Virtue As the Sole Good

According to Stoics, the only true good is virtue (made up of wisdom, courage, justice, and temperance), and everything else, including reputation, is "indifferent." This doesn't mean that reputation is unimportant, but it should not override your moral choices. As Epictetus advocates, "Attach yourself to what is spiritually superior, regardless of what other people think or do. Hold to your true aspirations no matter what is going on around you."

Authenticity over Approval

Stoicism values living authentically according to rational principles over seeking approval or praise from others. This encourages individuals to act according to their true nature and convictions rather than performing for social approval. Seneca keenly teaches that a person should live up to their own values rather than taking actions to become popular. "It takes trickery to win popular approval," he writes. "And you must needs make yourself like unto them; they will withhold their approval if they do not recognize you as one of themselves. However, what you think of yourself is much more to the point than what others think of you."

Reputation As a Tool

While Stoics advocated for indifference to reputation, they also recognized the role of social duties. A Stoic maintains their reputation only insofar as it helps them fulfill their social and moral duties effectively. They may also maintain their reputation if it potentially aids in achieving significant objectives, like influencing others positively or facilitating virtuous actions. You can apply Epictetus's teachings about the correct use of external things; he says: "Getting those things is not in my control—and not good or bad in any case. But the way I use them is good or bad, and depends on me."

Negative Feedback As a Gift

From a Stoic viewpoint, criticism or a "bad" reputation can be constructive if it is true. Epictetus remarks, "If evil be spoken of you and it be true, correct yourself, if it's a lie, laugh at it." Learning to view what others say about you objectively provides an opportunity to reflect and improve. If what others have to say about you is incorrect, then you can dig deeper to see if maybe you have been misunderstood and reach out with compassion.

The Freedom of Low Expectations

There's a counterintuitive freedom in being underestimated or having a less prominent reputation. Worrying less about your reputation may reduce pressure and external distractions, allowing you to focus more on personal growth and less on maintaining public image.

Focus on Process

The Stoic idea of focusing on process over outcomes can be applied to your reputation. As Epictetus teaches, "If you wish to be well spoken of, learn to speak well (of others): and when you have learned to speak well of them, try to act well, and so you will reap the fruit of being well spoken of." By living in accordance with virtue, you can focus on what you can control, and let the result be what it will be. Ironically, worrying less about your reputation and focusing on having integrity increases the likelihood of developing a good reputation. As Musonius Rufus observes, "You will earn the respect of all if you begin by earning the respect of yourself."

Learning to care less about what others think of you is challenging. Adopting a more Stoic perspective on reputation and focusing on internal virtues and rationality over external opinions can lead to greater personal freedom and authenticity.

DEALING WITH CRITICISM

Stoicism and Welcoming Feedback

Quotable Voices

"For what does reason purport to do? 'Establish what is true, eliminate what is false and suspend judgment in doubtful cases.' ... What else does reason prescribe? 'To accept the consequence of what has been admitted to be correct.'"

—Epictetus

Everyone faces criticism in their lives. Whether it's feedback from work, complaints from a romantic partner, or even gossip from friends, negative feedback is unavoidable. However, Stoicism's approach to handling criticism provides an opportunity to explore how you can use this philosophy to develop resilience, perspective, and growth.

STOIC TOOLS TO HANDLING CRITICISM

Consider some of the useful tools offered by Stoicism to handle criticism and still keep your cool.

Perception and Reaction

Stoicism teaches that a person's reaction to external events, including criticism, is based on their perceptions, which they can control. Criticism, no matter how harsh, does not inherently affect you unless you allow it to. "What, for instance, does it mean to be insulted?" asks Epictetus. "Stand by a rock and insult it, and what have you accomplished? If someone responds to insult like a rock, what has the abuser gained with his invective?"

Dichotomy of Control

Related to the first point, this fundamental Stoic principle asserts that one should focus only on what is within one's control—one's thoughts, feelings, and actions. External opinions and events, like criticism, are beyond your control and should be met with indifference in terms of emotional impact. Epictetus teaches that people must remain indifferent to what others say about them to not be controlled by others: "Any person capable of angering you becomes your master; he can anger you only when you permit yourself to be disturbed by him."

Role of Reason

Rational analysis is crucial in the Stoic response to criticism. When receiving criticism, it is easy for a person to feel insulted by someone pointing out a weakness or failure. By using Stoic objectivity and assessing whether the criticism is constructive, you can take that criticism as a useful data point for self-improvement. If the criticism is unfounded, it should be dismissed without emotional disturbance.

Opportunities for Growth

Stoics viewed adversity and criticism as opportunities to practice patience, humility, and resilience. "If you want to improve, be content to be thought foolish and stupid," says Epictetus, teaching that to learn, a person needs to be humble. By practicing humility, rather than reacting to criticism, each challenge is a chance to strengthen your character and adherence to Stoic principles. Epictetus also teaches people to be open to the possibility that they might be wrong or ignorant: "It is impossible for a man to learn what he thinks he already knows."

Welcoming Criticism

As emperor, Marcus Aurelius was continually looking for ways to improve himself, valuing truth over ego. "If someone can prove me wrong and show me my mistake in any thought or action," he writes, "I shall gladly change. I seek the truth, which never harmed anyone: the harm is to persist in one's own self-deception and ignorance."

While most might naturally shy away from or react negatively to criticism, Stoics encouraged people to welcome it. Criticism provides a unique perspective that reveals unspotted deficiencies or areas for improvement, making it a valuable tool for personal growth. As Seneca cleverly says, "A gem cannot be polished without friction, nor a man perfected without trials."

Take Things Lightly

Epictetus floats the idea of taking things lightly: "If someone speaks badly of you, do not defend yourself against the accusations, but reply, 'You obviously don't know about my other vices, otherwise you would have mentioned these as well.'" When you realize that everyone has shortcomings, you can take criticism without it disturbing your equanimity. Epictetus gives a compelling reason to not take oneself too seriously when he quips, "He who laughs at himself never runs out of things to laugh at."

Indifference to Praise and Criticism

Stoics strove to be indifferent not only to criticism but also to praise; both are seen as externals that should not influence one's inner peace and self-worth. This approach can be unconventional in a culture that often seeks and values external validation. Marcus Aurelius observes, "A thing is neither better nor worse for having been praised," reminding himself that receiving accolades doesn't change one's inherent value.

Ego

Criticism is often hard to receive because it brushes up against your inner view of yourself. Your ego may feel attacked when others point out where you might be deficient. This inconsistency can often lead you to act defensively or lash out in anger. Epictetus advises that a person consider the following when dealing with criticism: "Consider him with whom you converse in one of these three ways: either as your superior, or inferior, or equal. If superior, you ought to hear him and be convinced; if inferior, to convince him; if equal, to agree with him; and thus you will never be led into the love of strife." If you are able to approach any situation humbly and with an openness to learn and grow, you're less likely to have conflict with others.

Giving Criticism

On the other hand, you need to consider how you give feedback and criticism to others. Socrates advises that before a person speaks, they should consider the following: "Is it true; is it kind, or is it necessary?" By using these criteria, you can evaluate if what you say is helpful or if it should be said at all. Epictetus echoes this sentiment, saying, "Let silence be your general rule; or say only what is necessary and in few words."

Stoicism provides practical and profound strategies for dealing with criticism, emphasizing rational evaluation, humility, and the pursuit of virtue. From a Stoic perspective, feedback of any kind can be a useful tool for self-improvement and growth.

NO OPINION

Let Go of Your Judgments

Everyone has opinions about many things in the world, but the Stoics taught that there are times when opinions should be withheld or are simply unnecessary. Whether it is because something is inconsequential, none of your business, or you simply don't have enough information, holding off on making a judgment can often be the wisest course of action.

STOIC VIEWS ON OPINIONS

Check out Stoicism's view on opinions and judgments.

Nature of Judgment

"It is in our power to have no opinion about a thing and not to be disturbed in our soul; for things themselves have no natural power to form our judgments," penned Marcus Aurelius, teaching that external things are neutral, and that one's judgments about them are created from one's own perspective. Stoicism teaches that judgments are the primary source of distress, not the events themselves. As Epictetus says, "When then we are impeded or disturbed or grieved, let us never blame others, but ourselves, that is, our opinions." In this passage, Epictetus explains the importance of distinguishing between objective events and one's subjective interpretations.

The Power of Suspension

Suspending judgment and pausing before forming an opinion to assess whether a judgment is necessary or correct, and what value it adds to your life, is a powerful Stoic tool.

"You can process in your intellect and senses a wealth of thoughts and impressions simultaneously," Epictetus explains. "There are impressions that you assent to, others that you reject; sometimes you suspend judgment altogether."

This passage is saying a person should take their time before making judgments when they perceive something. (For more on the topics of impression and assent, see the Impressions and Assent section.)

Cato the Younger, known for his calm and rational demeanor, states, "The wise man considers in silence whatever anyone says." By taking the time to choose your response rather than reacting in a situation, you are more likely to make a wise judgment, or simply choose not to make one at all.

Impact on Emotions

By withholding judgments, especially hasty ones, you can maintain emotional equilibrium. This Stoic practice helps prevent unnecessary emotions like anger, resentment, or disappointment. Marcus Aurelius writes about the power of this approach: "You always own the option of having no opinion. There is never any need to get worked up or to trouble your soul about things you can't control. These things are not asking to be judged by you. Leave them alone."

Rationality and Open-Mindedness

"I know that I am intelligent, because I know that I know nothing," says Socrates, teaching the importance of approaching any situation from a place of ignorance as a way to not let your preexisting opinions get in the way of seeing things clearly. Letting go of judgments enhances rational thinking by allowing you to observe and interact with the world more objectively, promoting mental clarity and reducing biases.

Strength in Indecision

In a society that values quick decisions and strong opinions, choosing not to form an opinion can be seen as a weakness. However, Stoics viewed this as a strength, emphasizing that often the wisest decision is to reserve judgment. Cato the Younger advises restraint before speaking, saying, "I will begin to speak, when I have that to say which had not better be unsaid."

Emotional Neutrality As Engagement

Contrary to the idea that emotional engagement is necessary for a meaningful experience, Stoics argued that emotional neutrality can lead to deeper understanding and engagement. By practicing neutrality, you can see situations more clearly without the cloud of intense emotions, allowing you to engage with others from a place of curiosity and understanding, rather than trying to defend your opinions.

Finding Freedom in Detachment

Letting go of judgments can seem like detachment from the world, but Stoics found freedom in this detachment. It allows for a more adaptable and less reactive approach to life's challenges and maintains control over one's emotions, rather than being controlled by external events. As Epictetus teaches, "We, not externals, are the masters of our judgments."

PRACTICAL APPLICATIONS OF THINKING ABOUT OPINIONS

Stoics' views of expressing opinions are seen in the following practical applications.

Corporate Decision-Making

A business leader who practices Stoicism might delay forming opinions on new market trends or employee feedback until comprehensive data is analyzed, demonstrating the strength in reserved judgment.

Interpersonal Relationships

In personal relationships, practicing Stoics might choose to withhold negative judgments about others' actions, leading to fewer conflicts and deeper understanding. By reserving judgment and taking your time in considering alternative explanations for those actions, you may be better able to approach the situation with kindness and compassion, leading to understanding and enhancing connections.

MODERN EXAMPLES OF STOIC VIEWS OF OPINIONS

Consider the following modern examples of Stoicism's views on opinions.

John F. Kennedy

In 1962, during the Cuban Missile Crisis, President John F. Kennedy faced unprecedented pressure to react militarily against Soviet missile installations in Cuba. Instead of making hasty decisions, Kennedy took time to explore all available options and communicate with Soviet Union leaders, ultimately negotiating a peaceful resolution that avoided nuclear war.

Jacinda Ardern

After the tragic mosque shootings in Christchurch, New Zealand, in 2019, Prime Minister Jacinda Ardern responded with notable composure and empathy. She took the time to formulate responses that not only addressed the immediate crisis but also brought the country together.

Forming judgments is an aspect of human nature that often leads to divisiveness and discord. Stoic practices of suspending judgment not only lead to personal tranquility but also encourage more thoughtful, rational, and compassionate interactions with others.

RESILIENCE

What Stands in the Way Becomes the Way

Quotable Voices

"The mind adapts and converts to its own purposes the obstacle to our acting. The impediment to action advances action. What stands in the way becomes the way."

—Marcus Aurelius

In the grand theater of life, where you often find yourself playing the role of the bewildered protagonist, Stoicism teaches that the obstacles one encounters aren't just inconvenient plot twists but are, in fact, the plot itself. Obstacles and hardships aren't the things keeping you from getting what you want; rather, they are the things that strengthen you and give you the skills needed to get what you want. The obstacle *is* the way.

Philosophical Definition

resilience: The Stoics defined resilience as the capacity to endure and adapt to adversity or suffering through a disciplined use of reason while maintaining inner tranquility and virtue, regardless of external circumstances. It involves the steadfast commitment to act in accordance with nature and reason, viewing challenges as opportunities for growth and self-improvement.

OBSTACLES

"The trials you encounter will introduce you to your strengths. Remain steadfast . . . and one day you will build something that endures: something worthy of your potential," declares Epictetus, suggesting that every obstacle is not so much a roadblock as a personal trainer in disguise, challenging a person to push a little harder. Imagine a boxer who only fights easier, less trained opponents. While the boxer may have a winning record, they never improve their skills and never move up the ranks into the tougher and more prestigious bouts. Having more challenging opponents forces the boxer to be swifter on their feet, avoid their opponents' blows, and learn how to land that stinging right hook.

Seneca, who was as much a dramatist as he was a philosopher, knew the art of spinning a good yarn out of life's trials. He says, "Difficulties strengthen the mind, as labor does the body." It's the ancient Stoic equivalent of "What doesn't kill you makes you stronger." It's a call to embrace challenge, not because you enjoy struggle but because you recognize the strength, wisdom, and resilience it can build. Without challenges, there would be no growth.

Marcus Aurelius famously stated, "Just as nature takes every obstacle, every impediment, and works around it—turns it to its purposes, incorporates it into itself—so, too, a rational being can turn each setback into raw material and use it to achieve its goal." This is a central tenet of Stoicism: the importance of one's responses to external circumstances. While a person can't control every aspect of their life, they have the autonomy to choose their reactions. This empowers them to approach obstacles with a mindset geared toward growth and improvement, rather than defeat and frustration.

Epictetus himself was an excellent example of how to apply resilience in one's life. Born enslaved, he was once severely beaten by his master, breaking his leg and leaving him with a lifelong limp. Despite having these two strikes against him, Epictetus became one of the most influential Stoic philosophers with prominent figures seeking his advice, including Emperor Hadrian, and he was mentioned in *Meditations* by Marcus Aurelius as an important influence on his life.

CHARACTER

The Stoics weren't suggesting people seek out difficulties for their sake (they were philosophers, not masochists), but they also recognized that it is impossible to escape challenges in life. The Stoics believed the only good is the cultivation of virtue, meaning that the only important thing in life is the development of good character. Therefore, anything outside of oneself—events and circumstances, opinions of others, beauty, health, and wealth—was considered neither good nor bad but things to help one to develop virtue. In essence, it's not possible to develop virtue in a vacuum, but you can develop it by getting in the ring and giving it your best.

It's a logical approach. How do you know if you are being wise if you never have anything to practice your wisdom against? How do you know if you are courageous if you avoid all the difficult situations in your life? It is only through trying to apply wisdom by making difficult choices or being courageous and standing up to a bully that a person knows if they are developing their virtue.

EMOTIONAL RESILIENCE

This isn't just about finding a silver lining in every cloud; it's about seeing the cloud as essential to the landscape. Stoicism doesn't ask people to suppress their feelings or pretend everything's peachy when it's clearly a pear-shaped disaster. Instead, it invites people to acknowledge their emotions, take a deep breath, and then choose a response that aligns with their values and long-term goals. It's about recognizing that while you can't control what happens to you, you have the power to control your perceptions and reactions. This realization is both liberating and empowering, like discovering a cheat code in the game of life.

Incorporating Stoicism into your life means seeing every challenge as a personal trainer, tasked with strengthening your resilience muscles. Lost your job? Here's an opportunity to explore new paths. Facing criticism? A chance to practice grace and maybe learn something valuable. The Stoics asserted that life's obstacles aren't just hurdles to overcome; they're part of the curriculum in the school of life, teaching a person lessons they didn't know they needed.

Stoicism offers a unique perspective on life's challenges. By embracing the idea that "what stands in the way becomes the way," Stoics transformed their relationship with obstacles, seeing these barriers as integral to their growth and success. The obstacle isn't blocking your path—it *is* the path.

STOICISM AND GOALS

Opportunities for Growth

Quotable Voices
"Seek not the good in external things; seek it in yourselves."
—Epictetus

Stoicism can be useful for setting and achieving personal goals in life, aligning practical ambition with ethical integrity. A Stoic embraces whatever outcome their performance yields, focusing instead on their personal best and integrity.

SETTING GOALS THE STOIC WAY

Here are a few things to consider when setting goals from a Stoic perspective.

Virtue As the Primary Goal

Musonius Rufus writes, "If you accomplish something good with hard work, the labor passes quickly, but the good endures; if you do something shameful in pursuit of pleasure, the pleasure passes quickly, but the shame endures." In Stoicism, the primary goal is to live a life of virtue—being wise, just, courageous, and temperate. Goals related to external achievements are seen as "preferred indifferents." Achieving wealth or fame, for example, would be considered acceptable as long as these goals contribute to a virtuous life.

Process over Outcome

Stoics focused on the process of action rather than the outcome. They emphasized that how one works toward achieving one's goal, such as achieving success ethically, is more important than the result, which they believed is not entirely within one's control. As Epictetus clearly explains: "Show me one person who cares how they act, someone for whom success is less important than the manner in which it is achieved. While out walking, who gives any thought to the act of walking itself? Who pays attention to the process of planning, not just the outcome?"

Internal versus External Goals

Stoicism teaches that true fulfillment comes from internal states (such as virtue and wisdom) rather than external circumstances (such as wealth or success). This perspective encourages setting goals that refine one's character and virtue. The Stoics would argue that the highest goals are those entirely within one's own power to achieve—namely, self-improvement and virtue.

Setting Goals As a Path for Improvement

"Not to assume it's impossible because you find it hard. But to recognize that if it's humanly possible, you can do it too," Marcus Aurelius writes, urging that one not shy away from things that are difficult, but embrace them. The Stoics would assert that working toward challenging goals can be a path for self-discovery and improvement and can reveal hidden strengths that one might previously have been unaware of. As Epictetus teaches, "Circumstances don't make the man, they only reveal him to himself."

For example, taking on a more challenging role at work can be an opportunity for improving your skills or developing new ones.

Adopting a more rigorous exercise routine can be seen as a way to step out of your comfort zone and push yourself past previous limits. "Flee laziness, because the indolence of the soul is the decay of the body," says Cato the Younger, encouraging hard work and productivity in society.

Adaptability and Acceptance

Stoics advocated for setting goals while also being prepared to accept any outcome with equanimity. A person should adopt a flexible approach to goals, adjusting them as needed based on circumstances beyond one's control.

Practicing Stoic acceptance means that you need to accept that some goals may not be possible for you to achieve due to circumstances beyond your control. For example, someone might be an excellent basketball player but may not have the physical height necessary to play in the NBA.

Embracing Failure As Success

"A setback has often cleared the way for greater prosperity. Many things have fallen only to rise to more exalted heights," writes Seneca as a reminder that setbacks need not derail a person from working toward their goals. Stoics viewed apparent failures as opportunities to practice virtues such as resilience and humility and to develop new strengths. Therefore, a Stoic would set a goal fully aware of the potential for failure, valuing the opportunity for growth that the challenge represents, regardless of the outcome. In short, striving for your goals can develop your character and allow you the chance to achieve what you'd set out to do.

Detachment from Desires

Stoicism promotes a form of goal setting that is somewhat detached from the desires that typically drive ambitions. This means pursuing objectives while remaining indifferent to the pleasure or pain their achievement or non-achievement may bring. Marcus Aurelius writes, "Receive wealth or prosperity without arrogance; and be ready to let it go." This quote serves as a reminder that you should not be attached to your successes or failures.

Patience and Consistency

"No great thing is created suddenly, any more than a bunch of grapes or a fig," says Epictetus. "If you tell me that you desire a fig, I answer that there must be time. Let it first blossom, then bear fruit, then ripen." This passage indicates that your desires and achievements are not acquired overnight. Practicing patience and consistency is something you need to develop to improve. As Epictetus teaches, "We should discipline ourselves in small things, and from there progress to things of greater value."

MODERN EXAMPLES OF SETTING GOALS

The following are modern Stoic examples of setting goals.

Keanu Reeves

Known for his humble lifestyle and philosophical outlook, Reeves often displays indifference toward Hollywood's glamorous lifestyle and focuses more on personal growth and helping others. His approach to fame and adversity—with calm and generosity—mirrors Stoic ideals.

Tom Brady

Attributed to his meticulous diet, exercise routines, and mental training, Brady's career longevity in the physically demanding NFL is a testament to his disciplined approach to maintaining peak physical condition and mental resilience. His focus on controllable factors, such as his training regime and attitude, rather than an obsession with winning, aligns with Stoic principles.

Stoicism provides robust principles for setting and pursuing goals that ensure personal growth and integrity instead of mere external success. This approach not only leads to more sustainable achievements but also to profound personal satisfaction and resilience.

MORAL CONSISTENCY

The Power of Stoic Integrity

Stoicism advocates unwavering adherence to ethical principles in all circumstances. A person should hold to their principles and beliefs not only when it is easy but, more importantly, when it is difficult. Committing to regular practice of one's morals is a key part of Stoicism.

Philosophical Definition

moral consistency: Moral consistency refers to the adherence to the same set of ethical principles across different situations, regardless of personal feelings, social pressures, or potential consequences. It means aligning one's actions, decisions, and judgments consistently with these ethical standards, demonstrating a steadfast commitment to these values over time and in all circumstances.

STOIC CONSISTENCY

Consistency is the key to progress in any area of life, especially in self-development. By remaining vigilant, you can ensure your thoughts and actions consistently align with Stoic principles. Read on to explore some ways that you can practice Stoic consistency.

Maintaining Integrity

When the Stoics spoke about moral consistency, they meant that a person consistently maintains their own integrity over time. A person who is morally consistent acts in accordance with their own beliefs and values at all times, in public and in private, without regard to the potential for personal gain or loss. As Epictetus explains, "Settle on the type of person you want to be and stick to it, whether alone or in company." Simply put, moral consistency means that you "talk the talk, and walk the walk."

Virtue As the Sole Good

Epictetus states, "Attach yourself to what is spiritually superior, regardless of what other people think or do. Hold to your true aspirations no matter what is going on around you." Stoicism teaches that virtue—wisdom, justice, courage, and temperance—is the only true good. Moral consistency arises from prioritizing these virtues above all else, regardless of the consequences.

Continuous Evaluation

Regular self-examination and reflection on one's actions and motives ensure alignment with Stoic virtues. Marcus Aurelius suggests that one check in with oneself before acting or speaking: "If it is not right, do not do it: if it is not true, do not say it. For let your impulse be in your own power."

Moral Autonomy

Stoicism teaches that moral authority lies entirely within oneself, not in societal norms or laws. This can lead to choices that defy conventional expectations but are consistent with one's own ethical principles. This is especially important in positions of power in business and public office, where ample opportunities for personal enrichment or profit using unethical or illegal means exist. By maintaining moral integrity, you can keep a clear conscience and preserve your composure, avoiding the guilt and shame of unethical action. Epictetus teaches, "Happiness and personal fulfillment are the natural consequences of doing the right thing."

Indifference to Externals

Epictetus teaches what a person should ask themselves to not let external events influence their actions: "How do I handle chance impressions, naturally or unnaturally? Do I respond to them as I should, or don't I? Do I tell externals that they are nothing to me?" Stoics maintained that external factors such as wealth, success, and even health are "indifferents." These factors can be preferred or unpreferred but should never compromise one's moral integrity.

Rational Control over Emotions

Stoics argued that emotions result from judgments about what is good or bad. With training, a person can suspend immediate judgments and see external events as neutral. By doing these things, a person maintains moral clarity and consistency. Marcus Aurelius reflects, "Everywhere, at each moment, you have the option: to accept this event with humility; to treat this person as he should be treated; to approach this thought with care, so that nothing irrational creeps in." In other words, you always have the option of doing the good thing, and the implication is that you should do it.

Embracing Adversity for Growth

Unlike the common tendency to avoid difficulties, the Stoics viewed adversity as a fertile ground for practicing and strengthening virtue. As Seneca says, "It does not matter what you bear, but how you bear it." Challenges are seen as opportunities to demonstrate and reinforce moral consistency.

Detachment from Outcomes

It might seem counterintuitive, but the Stoics advocated for detachment from the outcomes of one's actions. This detachment allows individuals to focus on acting virtuously without being swayed by potential rewards or punishments. Marcus Aurelius plainly states, "Just that you do the right thing. The rest doesn't matter."

Service

Cato the Younger says, "The best way to keep good acts in memory is to refresh them with new," advising people to actively seek out opportunities to do good in the world. The Stoic concept of cosmopolitanism, that every individual is a citizen of the world, means that you find ways to serve those outside of your immediate circle of friends and family.

MODERN EXAMPLES OF
MORAL CONSISTENCY

Stoicism's moral consistency is demonstrated in the following modern examples.

Malala Yousafzai

Despite being attacked for advocating girls' education, Malala continued her activism without compromising her principles. Her moral consistency in the face of life-threatening adversity exemplifies Stoic courage and justice.

Patagonia, Inc.

Patagonia, Inc., consistently places environmental sustainability and ethical practices at the core of its business, even when it might be economically disadvantageous. This commitment reflects a Stoic-like adherence to virtue (in this case, justice and moderation) over profit. By actually putting their principles into practice rather than just paying them lip service, Patagonia, Inc., is following Seneca's admonition "It is difficult to bring people to goodness with lessons, but it is easy to do so by example," and they are showing that a company can act ethically and be profitable.

Stoicism equips individuals to maintain moral consistency through rational thought, emotional management, and a profound commitment to virtue. By adhering to Stoic moral consistency, individuals and organizations can navigate ethical dilemmas and maintain integrity in complex modern contexts.

PREMEDITATIO MALORUM

Why Imagining the Worst Can Help You Be Your Best

While the Stoics were keen on being in the present moment as much as possible, they also understood that people needed to plan for the possible challenges that might come their way. The concept of *Premeditatio Malorum* is another tool in the Stoic toolbox for reducing anxiety of those future events.

Philosophical Definition

Premeditatio Malorum: A Latin term meaning "the premeditation of evils." It encompasses the idea that one should consider the worst possible outcomes in order to not be surprised or overwhelmed should they occur.

WHAT'S THE WORST THAT COULD HAPPEN?

Premeditatio Malorum is a particularly powerful tool to prepare for the possible downturns of life. It involves the practice of visualizing potential adversities to prepare oneself emotionally and mentally for difficult times. It's like developing a disaster response mindset to your life, so that you can be mentally prepared for the worst-case scenario. As Seneca clearly explains, "The person who has anticipated the coming of troubles takes away their power when they arrive."

HOW TO PRACTICE
PREMEDITATIO MALORUM

In his *Moral Letters to Lucilius*, Seneca gives a basic explanation of how to put *Premeditatio Malorum* into practice:

"We need to envisage every possibility and to strengthen the spirit to deal with the things which may conceivably come about. Rehearse them in your mind: exile, torture, war, shipwreck. Misfortune may snatch you away from your country. . . . If we do not want to be overwhelmed and struck numb by rare events as if they were unprecedented ones; fortune needs envisaging in a thoroughly comprehensive way."

—Seneca

By contemplating events such as a loss of wealth, an illness, or the death of loved ones, a person can prepare for and accept these as natural occurrences. This exercise is a deliberate practice to help mitigate the shock and pain that might otherwise overwhelm an unprepared mind.

PRACTICAL APPLICATIONS OF
PREMEDITATIO MALORUM

There are many practical applications of *Premeditatio Malorum*, as explained in the following paragraphs.

Dealing with Other People

Marcus Aurelius writes, "When you wake up in the morning, tell yourself: The people I deal with today will be meddling, ungrateful, arrogant, dishonest, jealous, and surly. They are like this because they can't tell good from evil." This teaching was a reminder to himself that in his duties as emperor, he would deal with difficult people and would need to prepare to treat them with compassion. Start each day by contemplating a few potential minor misfortunes, such as being stuck in traffic or dealing with a difficult coworker. This way you handle them with composure.

Dealing with Grief

Seneca writes about the transient nature of life and loved ones every day:

"Remember that all we have is 'on loan' from Fortune, which can reclaim it without our permission—indeed, without even advance notice. Thus, we should love all our dear ones, but always with the thought that we have no promise that we may keep them forever—nay, no promise even that we may keep them for long."

—Seneca

By remembering that death comes for everyone, you can appreciate others in your life and prepare for their loss with strength and courage.

The Fickleness of Fortune

Seneca notes that success and wealth can be easily won and easily lost, advising, "In the meantime, cling tooth and nail to the following rule: not to give in to adversity, not to trust prosperity, and always take full note of fortune's habit of behaving just as she pleases."

Focus on Virtue

"Keep death and exile before your eyes each day, along with everything that seems terrible—by doing so, you'll never have a base thought nor will you have excessive desire," says Epictetus, as a way to focus on living a life of virtue. By thinking through how you would handle challenging situations, you are better able to act according to your principles when those situations arise.

BENEFITS OF *PREMEDITATIO MALORUM*

There are many benefits of *Premeditatio Malorum*, including the following.

Reduced Anxiety

The practice of *Premeditatio Malorum* is not about ruminating on everything that could go wrong but instead a deliberate, thoughtful, and detached mental process. By continuously exposing the mind to potential negative outcomes, one becomes less likely to be unsettled when they happen.

Increased Gratitude

Regular contemplation of worst-case scenarios makes a person more appreciative of their current circumstances. It's the Stoic version of the idea that it could always be worse, but with a positive purpose.

Enhanced Problem-Solving

Seneca writes, "I look for the best and am prepared for the opposite," as a simple reminder of how to approach challenges. Since most things don't go according to plan, thinking about what could go wrong forces a person to come up with solutions in advance, which can be applied to real-life situations. You can see this practice put into action in disaster response teams, the training of surgeons, and even corporate IT teams.

Premeditatio Malorum is more than just rumination on the bad things that could happen; it is a preparation for life's inevitable difficulties. It embodies the Stoic ideal of not being surprised by the misfortunes of life but instead embracing them with readiness and dignity. By integrating this practice into daily life, you can fortify yourself against the shocks and stresses of the human condition and live with greater tranquility and effectiveness.

GRATITUDE
Want What You Have

Quotable Voices

"He is a wise man who does not grieve for the things which he
has not, but rejoices for those which he has."

—Epictetus

In a world that promotes happiness through acquiring wealth and
possessions, Stoic philosophy proposes that one find contentment
by mindfully practicing gratitude for what one already has. Rather
than seeking fulfillment for future success or acquiring more possessions, you can reduce your desires and find happiness in your
present circumstances.

STOIC CONTENTMENT

Stoic contentment is all about recognizing what is already good in
your life, and even appreciating the challenges you have as opportunities to grow.

Virtue and Contentment

Stoicism teaches that true happiness comes from virtue and that
external circumstances can neither add nor subtract from this happiness. Gratitude in Stoicism is therefore about appreciating life as
it is, not as one wishes it to be. As Seneca teaches, "No person has
the power to have everything they want, but it is in their power not

to want what they don't have, and to cheerfully put to good use what they do have."

Negative Visualization

The Stoic practice of negative visualization involves imagining losing what one has—not to foster fear but to enhance appreciation for those things while they are still present. As Seneca explains, "No good thing renders its possessor happy, unless his mind is reconciled to the possibility of loss; nothing, however, is lost with less discomfort than that which, when lost, cannot be missed." By rehearsing how you would feel about the loss of your possessions, your career, and even your loved ones, you can enjoy and appreciate them more while you have them, and be ready to handle their loss.

Detachment Enhances Gratitude

While it may seem paradoxical, the Stoic form of detachment—being indifferent to having or losing an external good—fosters a deeper appreciation for it. This doesn't mean a Stoic doesn't enjoy good things; a Stoic enjoys good things without attachment, enhancing that person's gratitude by not taking the good things for granted. Seneca muses about attachment to external things, "Until we have begun to go without them, we fail to realize how unnecessary many things are. We've been using them not because we needed them but because we had them."

Appreciation of Simple Things

With a focus on simplicity, Stoicism teaches that possessions and wealth should be treated as "indifferents," and that one should focus on internal virtues and simple pleasures. "Do not indulge in dreams of having what you have not, but reckon up the chief of the blessings you do possess, and then thankfully remember how you would crave for them if they were not yours," writes Marcus Aurelius in appreciation of what he had.

Mindfulness and Presence

"True happiness is to enjoy the present, without anxious dependence upon the future, not to amuse ourselves with either hopes or fears but to rest satisfied with what we have, which is sufficient, for he that is so wants nothing," writes Seneca as an advocation to appreciate the present moment. By worrying about the future, a person focuses on things that are outside of their control and on outcomes that might never come to pass. Epictetus encourages instead focusing on the present moment: "Caretake this moment. Immerse yourself in its particulars. Respond to this person, this challenge, this deed. Quit evasions. Stop giving yourself needless trouble. It is time to really live; to fully inhabit the situation you happen to be in now."

Gratitude for Difficulties

Stoics strove to maintain equanimity in the face of both good and bad external circumstances. The Stoic concept of *Amor Fati*, "to love one's fate," can be seen as practicing gratitude in positive and challenging moments alike. Stoics found value and reasons for gratitude in difficult circumstances and viewed challenges as opportunities to practice virtue and grow stronger.

Less Desire, More Happiness

In contrast to the idea that pursuing more possessions or achievements leads to increased happiness, Stoics found that reducing desires leads to greater satisfaction. Seneca observes, "If we could be satisfied with anything, we should have been satisfied long ago," noting that desires abound, and that even when a person acquires what they want, they are often still unsatisfied. Gratitude arises naturally when one wants less and appreciates what is already present. "Wealth," says Epictetus, "consists not in having great possessions, but in having few wants."

Stoics in Exile

Because of their outspoken views against those in power, many of the Stoics were sent into exile, but even in exile, they found contentment. Seneca, banished by Claudius, took the time to devote himself to writing and penned some of his most famous works. Musonius Rufus lived in exile three separate times and accepted his fate willingly. When responding to Thrasea, his sometimes ally in opposing Nero who said, "I would sooner be killed today than banished tomorrow," Rufus responded, "If you choose death because it is the greater evil, what sense is there in that? Or if you choose it as the lesser-evil, remember who gave you the choice. Why not try coming to terms with what you have been given?" Regardless of circumstances, these Stoics made the best of their situations and found ways to be grateful and helpful.

MODERN APPLICATION OF GRATITUDE

The following are some modern applications of gratitude.

Minimalism

The modern minimalist movement echoes Stoic principles—people find greater joy and gratitude by reducing their possessions to what is essential, thereby focusing on what truly adds value to their lives. By embracing the idea that you don't own your possessions but rather they own you, minimalism echoes the teachings of Seneca. He says, "As far as I am concerned, I know that I have lost not wealth but distractions."

Modern Gratitude

Modern celebrities, such as Oprah Winfrey, frequently discuss the role of gratitude in their life, focusing on what they value rather than what they lack. Even those with great wealth can practice being grateful for what they have and find contentment in their lives.

Stoicism focuses on reducing one's desires, valuing simplicity, and appreciating internal virtue. This philosophy enriches the understanding of gratitude by shifting the emphasis from noticing what you lack to appreciating what you have, thereby promoting a more fulfilled and content life.

CONSISTENCY
Work On Yourself Daily

Quotable Voices
"What does Socrates say? 'One person likes tending to his farm, another to his horse; I like to daily monitor my self-improvement.'"
—Epictetus

The Stoics advocated a practice of daily self-improvement, with a focus on consistency to ensure that a person doesn't just learn about how to live a life of virtue; they also apply what they have learned. As Epictetus aptly notes, "That's why the philosophers warn us not to be satisfied with mere learning, but to add practice and then training. For as time passes we forget what we learned and end up doing the opposite, and hold opinions the opposite of what we should."

CONSISTENCY IS KEY

Learning about concepts for self-improvement is important, but without implementing them consistently, they are next to worthless. The Stoics provided some ways that you can consistently apply what you've learned.

Daily Practices

Stoicism advocates for daily routines and practices that rein-force discipline, mindfulness, and ethical living. This could include mental practices such as journaling, studying, and meditation, and physical practices such as exercise, eating simple meals, and fasting.

You could also review your actions at the end of the day to assess alignment with Stoic virtues.

The Role of Habits

Epictetus extolls, "Progress is not achieved by luck or accident, but by working on yourself daily." Stoics believed that virtue is a habit rather than a single act. Consistent daily practice helps develop habits of mind and behavior that lead to a virtuous and fulfilling life. As Marcus Aurelius advises, "Such as are your habitual thoughts, such also will be the character of your mind; for the soul is dyed by the thoughts. Dye it then with a continuous series of such thoughts as these: for instance, that where a man can live, there he can also live well."

Incremental Progress

Stoicism values small, consistent steps over sporadic leaps and suggests that true improvement comes from gradual, consistent effort rather than occasional moments of intensity. Epictetus understood that to improve, one needs patience and consistency: "No great thing is created suddenly, any more than a bunch of grapes or a fig. If you tell me that you desire a fig, I answer that there must be time. Let it first blossom, then bear fruit, then ripen."

Seize the Present Moment

The Stoics often spoke about seizing the present moment, and that a person should be constantly examining themselves to evaluate how they can live with virtue at every moment. Seneca recommends, "Begin at once to live, and count each separate day as a separate life." If a person does this, they will remember the importance of upholding their principles each moment, rather than pushing off improvement into the future.

Epictetus, in speaking about the importance of living each day to the best of one's ability, says:

"Now is the time to get serious about living your ideals. How long can you afford to put off who you really want to be? Your nobler self cannot wait any longer. Put your principles into practice—now. Stop the excuses and the procrastination. This is your life! [. . .] Decide to be extraordinary and do what you need to do—now."

—Epictetus

Mindfulness

Stoicism advocates mindfulness in all that one does, so one can be sure that each of one's actions align with one's principles. Marcus Aurelius succinctly explains, "Concentrate every minute [. . .] on doing what's in front of you with precise and genuine seriousness, tenderly, willingly, with justice. And on freeing yourself from all other distractions."

Seek Out Others

The Stoics understood that developing virtue in oneself was not something that a person could achieve alone. The Stoics advocated that individuals need others to help them become the type of person they want to become. "Associate with people who are likely to improve you. Welcome those who you are capable of improving. The process is a mutual one: men learn as they teach," writes Seneca. This means that a person should surround themselves with those who are willing to support them in their quest for self-improvement and who are open to improving themselves.

Embrace Boredom

In an age that constantly seeks stimulation, Stoicism teaches the value of embracing simplicity and even boredom. Routine and repetitive practices are seen as opportunities to deepen understanding and strengthen discipline. Seneca routinely took time for himself to ponder his life and notes: "Nothing, to my way of thinking, is a better proof of a well-ordered mind than a man's ability to stop just where he is and pass some time in his own company."

Detachment from Outcomes

While many philosophies and modern self-help strategies focus on achieving specific outcomes, Stoicism teaches detachment from the results of one's efforts. "Show me one person who cares how they act, someone for whom success is less important than the manner in which it is achieved. While out walking, who gives any thought to the act of walking itself? Who pays attention to the process of planning, not just the outcome?" teaches Epictetus, underscoring that the process and daily commitment to virtue are valued more than specific achievements.

Incorporating daily Stoic practices of mindfulness, study, and constant self-examination creates a practical framework for self-improvement. This consistent and incremental approach not only fosters personal growth and virtue; it also equips you to handle life's challenges with grace and resilience.

MORNING AND EVENING REFLECTIONS

Practices for Knowing Yourself

Quotable Voices

"Retire into thyself. For nowhere either with more quiet or more freedom from trouble does a man retire than into his own soul."
—Marcus Aurelius

Stoic morning and evening reflections present an opportunity to practice self-awareness, reflect on ways to cultivate virtue, and reinforce philosophical commitments. Think of these reflections as opportunities to map out each morning where you want to go, and then reflect on the progress you've made (or not) each evening.

STOIC REFLECTIONS

Stoics had many intricate thoughts on reflecting, shown in the following examples.

Purpose of Reflections

Stoicism promotes the practice of self-reflection to increase self-awareness, improve decision-making, and align actions with Stoic virtues (wisdom, justice, courage, and temperance). Morning reflections set the tone for the day, while evening reflections provide an opportunity to review and assess the day's actions. Through practicing daily reflections, you can follow the advice of Epictetus:

"You become what you give your attention to. . . . If you yourself don't choose what thoughts and images you expose yourself to, someone else will."

Morning Intentions

Morning reflections center on anticipating challenges and setting intentions for how to handle them in accordance with Stoic principles. Seneca writes, "As each day arises, welcome it as the very best day of all, and make it your own possession. We must seize what flees," as a reminder to start the day with purpose and intention. Adopting this proactive stance helps you prepare mentally and emotionally for the day ahead. As Seneca cleverly puts it, "If a man knows not which port he sails, no wind is favorable."

Evening Review

In the evening, the focus shifts to introspection and evaluation. This involves assessing one's actions throughout the day, acknowledging successes in applying Stoic principles, and identifying areas for improvement. Seneca, known for his diligence in self-reflection, explains this practice: "We should every night call ourselves to an account; What infirmity have I mastered today? What passions opposed? What temptation resisted? What virtue acquired? Our vices will abort of themselves if they be brought every day to the shrift." By reflecting on what took place that day, you become more mindful of what happened to you that day and how you responded to it.

Emotional Resilience

Regular reflections help build emotional resilience by fostering a habit of responding to situations with reason rather than impulsive emotions. Reflecting on one's emotional responses encourages a more deliberate and controlled approach to challenges. As Epictetus says, "Adopt new habits yourself: consolidate your principles by putting them into practice."

Embracing Discomfort

Stoicism teaches that discomfort and adversity are opportunities for growth. Morning reflections might include a deliberate anticipation of potential difficulties, not as threats but as chances to practice virtue. By practicing negative visualization of challenges they might face, a person is better prepared to handle those obstacles should they occur.

Building Habits

The Stoics were keen on building useful habits to reinforce their dedication to their principles. As Epictetus teaches, "If you like doing something, do it regularly; if you don't like doing something, make a habit of doing something different. The same goes for moral inclinations." By creating habits to increase your mindfulness, you are better able to handle any daily challenges in ways that align with your values.

Gratitude

Morning reflection can also include things that you are grateful for, helping set the tone for the day. "When you arise in the morning, think of what a precious privilege it is to be alive—to breathe, to think, to enjoy, to love," writes Marcus Aurelius. He encouraged focusing on the simple aspects of life because they're the things that one can derive happiness from, if one is willing to take the time and appreciate them.

Detachment from Success

While many personal development approaches emphasize celebrating successes, Stoic evening reflections focus more on the ethical execution of actions rather than the outcomes, leading to a deeper sense of fulfillment and detachment from external validations. Marcus Aurelius's *Meditations*, which focuses on his inner thoughts and reflection rather than listing off his conquests or political triumphs, is an excellent example of this practice.

Neutrality Toward Emotions

Contrary to many modern perspectives that encourage fully embracing one's emotions, the Stoics advocated observing emotions with a degree of detachment during daily reflections. This helps in understanding the emotions without being overwhelmed by them, promoting rational handling of future situations.

MODERN EXAMPLES OF REFLECTING

The following are modern examples of Stoicism's view of reflections.

Tim Ferriss

An entrepreneur, author, and public speaker, Tim Ferriss is an avid practitioner of journaling and meditation. He regularly discusses how daily reflection, particularly morning journaling, plays a crucial role in his ability to stay focused, make better decisions, and handle the stresses of his professional life. He credits these practices with helping him gain clarity and maintain productivity.

LeBron James

Professional basketball player LeBron James uses mindfulness and reflection practices to improve his mental focus. James has shared how meditation helps him stay at the top of his game mentally and physically, enabling him to perform under the intense pressure of professional sports.

Stoicism encourages people to develop self-awareness to aid in their quest for living in accordance with virtue. Incorporating Stoic morning and evening reflections into your life allows you to utilize practical tools for fostering self-improvement, emotional stability, and philosophical consistency in daily life.

STOIC THOUGHTS ON LOVE
Rationality and Affection

The Stoic perspective on love offers a unique insight on the complex nature of affection and relationships. Stoicism, with its emphasis on rational emotional management and compassion toward others, provides practical tools for maintaining healthy emotional bonds while pursuing personal and moral growth.

STOIC LOVE

Read on to explore ideas about love from a Stoic perspective.

Love As a Rational Affection

Marcus Aurelius, in writing about the importance of love, penned, "Accept the things to which fate binds you, and love the people with whom fate brings you together, but do so with all your heart." Stoics promoted the idea of love as a rational affection, which aligns with the virtues of wisdom and justice. Love, from a Stoic perspective, is not merely a passion or emotion; it is also a reasoned choice that involves wishing well for others and showing them kindness and respect.

Dichotomy of Control

The Stoic concept of the Dichotomy of Control, meaning clearly understanding what one does and does not have control over, can also be an effective tool in developing healthy relationships. By recognizing that you can only control your own actions, you are less likely to try to control your romantic partner's, leading to relationships of mutual respect and support. Epictetus reiterates this, teaching, "The object of your love is mortal; it is not one of your possessions."

Love and Attachment

Stoicism advocates for a form of love that is free from excessive attachment and dependency, maintaining a degree of emotional detachment even in close relationships. Stoics believed that true happiness does not depend on external factors, allowing them to love freely without fear of loss or disappointment. This can be helpful in setting healthy boundaries and resolving conflicts in a more productive and supportive manner.

Beneficial Love

Stoics argued that love should be beneficial to moral growth, and that love, when guided by virtue and rational principles, leads to healthy relationships that contribute positively to everyone's well-being. Seneca writes, "One of the most beautiful qualities of true friendship is to understand and to be understood." This means that any relationship, to be truly loving, must contribute to the moral and philosophical development of the people involved. Additionally, Epictetus teaches that through the development of virtue, one learns to love well: "If someone is incapable of distinguishing good things from bad and neutral things from either—well, how could such a person be capable of love? The power to love, then, belongs only to the wise man."

Embracing Impermanence

Unlike romantic notions that often emphasize "forever" aspects of love, Stoics embraced the impermanence of life and relationships. As Seneca explains, "We should love all our dear ones . . . but always with the thought that we have no promise that we may keep them forever—nay, no promise even that we may keep them for long." This acceptance of impermanence fosters a deeper appreciation for the present moments shared with loved ones.

Marriage and Children

The Stoics advocated for marriage and the raising of children as part of their duty as human beings and as a way to practice virtue. "So, in marriage there must be, above all, perfect companionship and mutual love—both in sickness, health and under all conditions—it should be with desire for this (and children) that both entered upon marriage," writes Musonius Rufus about the aspects that make a good marriage. Socrates, whose wife was apparently difficult to get along with, has a more humorous take on marriage, saying, "By all means marry; if you get a good wife, you'll become happy; if you get a bad one, you'll become a philosopher."

Many of the Stoics were devoted parents and saw children as a joy in their lives. Rufus, showing his sentimental side about parenting, notes, "What a great spectacle it is when a husband or wife with many children are seen with these children crowded around them!" Marcus Aurelius was known to be a devoted husband and father and suffered greatly at the loss of eight of his fourteen children. "From Sextus, [I learned] a benevolent disposition, and the example of a family governed in a fatherly manner, and the idea of living conformably to nature," writes Aurelius, noting the importance of being a good father and husband.

Romantic Love

The Stoics considered passions such as lust as negative emotions and, therefore, to be avoided. As Seneca notes, "Friendship always benefits; love sometimes injures." This was his reminder that overwhelming desire for a romantic partner can often cause distress, and that a person should work toward developing relationships built on friendship and trust. Musonius Rufus advocates openness and honesty between partners, writing, "Husband and wife should come together to craft a shared life, procreating children, seeing all things as shared between them—with nothing withheld or private to one another—not even their bodies."

Stoicism provides a nuanced and profound understanding of love, promoting relationships that are rational, respectful, and enriching. By applying Stoic principles, you can build relationships that support mutual personal growth, maintain independence while deepening emotional connections, and manage conflicts through rational discussion and reciprocal understanding.

STOIC OPTIMISM

Seeing the Bright Side

The Stoics are known for their reserve and emotional control, but underneath that calm exterior is an optimistic mindset about life. The Stoics maintained a hopeful and proactive attitude despite their realistic acknowledgment of life's challenges.

STOICALLY OPTIMISTIC

Stoic optimism may seem like an oxymoron, yet there are some ways that Stoic optimism can help brighten your day.

Rational Optimism

Stoicism promotes optimism based on the rational assessment of situations and self-confidence in dealing with them. This is different from indiscriminate optimism, or being heedlessly positive regardless of the situation. Stoics believed that a person could handle whatever life throws their way. This optimism is grounded in self-reliance and the belief in one's ability to maintain virtue in any circumstance. As Marcus Aurelius observes, "You can pass your life in an equable flow of happiness if you can follow the right way and think and act in the right way."

Optimism from Virtue

The Stoics posited that by living according to virtue, a person will naturally develop an optimistic disposition. In Seneca's words, "A man thus grounded must, whether he wills or not, necessarily be attended by constant cheerfulness and a joy that is deep and issues from deep within, since he finds delight in his own resources, and desires no joys greater than his inner joys."

Seneca proposed as well that living according to virtue helps a person to better deal with challenges of life while staying calm, writing, "Virtue alone affords everlasting and peace-giving joy; even if some obstacles arise, it is but like an intervening cloud, which floats beneath the sun but never prevails against it."

Role of Perception

Epictetus states, "Men are disturbed, not by things, but by the principles and notions which they form concerning things." Stoics believed that a person's reactions to events, rather than the events themselves, determine their experience. Optimism, therefore, comes from choosing to interpret life's events in ways that align with personal growth and virtue. Epictetus illustrates how this concept can be applied in all situations with a simple example: "Starting with things of little value—a bit of spilled oil, a little stolen wine—repeat to yourself: 'For such a small price I buy tranquility and peace of mind.'"

Control and Acceptance

Stoicism teaches the importance of distinguishing between what a person can and can't control. A person can find optimism when focusing on their own actions and attitudes and accepting they can't control everything, thus reducing unnecessary distress. Letting go of the desire to control everything leads to greater serenity and a positive, proactive focus on the things that one can actually influence.

Detachment from Outcomes

While many forms of optimism hinge on achieving desired outcomes, Stoic optimism is about being content regardless of how things turn out. This detachment from outcomes can paradoxically lead to greater mental freedom and happiness. "There is only one way to happiness," teaches Epictetus, "and that is to cease worrying about things which are beyond the power of our will."

Welcoming Obstacles

Stoics saw challenges as opportunities to strengthen character, which fosters a kind of optimism that values personal development over external circumstances. "The mind adapts and converts to its own purposes the obstacle to our acting. The impediment to action advances action. What stands in the way becomes the way," penned Marcus Aurelius as a reminder that obstacles should be embraced as paths to greater virtue and wisdom.

Amor Fati

The Stoic concept of *Amor Fati*, that a person should love everything that happens to them, is the ultimate form of optimism. By loving everything that happens to you, you cultivate a perspective that even hardships are valuable and can be used to your advantage. Epictetus teaches that by accepting things as they come, one can live a more peaceful life: "If we try to adapt our mind to the regular sequence of changes and accept the inevitable with good grace, our life will proceed quite smoothly and harmoniously."

Optimism in Negative Visualization

Seneca advises, "This is why we need to envisage every possibility and to strengthen the spirit to deal with the things which may conceivably come about." Stoics practiced *Premeditatio Malorum*, which involves contemplating potential negative outcomes. This practice might seem pessimistic, but it prepares the mind to face the worst, reducing future shocks and fostering a calm, confident, and optimistic approach when challenges arise.

Optimism about Human Nature

Despite acknowledging the flaws and irrationalities of human behavior, Stoics maintained a fundamentally optimistic view of human potential for reason and virtue. They believed that all people can achieve wisdom and goodness if they choose to live in accordance with nature. Marcus Aurelius urges, "If a man is mistaken, instruct him kindly and show him his error." In this way, offering compassion is just as important as spreading wisdom.

Gratitude

The Stoics advocated practicing gratitude to foster optimism. Marcus Aurelius reminded himself to be present and grateful for his life every morning. On a similar note, he writes, "Dwell on the beauty of life. Watch the stars, and see yourself running with them." His words may encourage you to take time to appreciate what you have and find beauty in the world around you.

Stoicism encourages an optimism that is not only enduring but also deeply empowering, enabling individuals to thrive in all circumstances by focusing on personal virtue, resilience, and gratitude.

INDEX

Acceptance, 33, 38, 43–60, 73, 87–88, 98, 107–9, 114–26, 143–93, 198–217, 232–48, 259–65

Acton, Lord John, 175

Adversity, 8, 39, 48, 56–59, 79–89, 117, 139–49, 186–87, 196, 200, 211, 218–26, 233–43, 256

Agrippinus, 211

Alexander the Great, 163

Amor Fati, 38, 88, 116, 143–46, 247, 265

Antonine Plague, 32, 96, 117, 132, 175

Antoninus, 28, 31, 148

Anxiety, 42–46, 83–89, 100, 112–19, 123–26, 137, 155, 165–74, 186, 240–44, 257

Apatheia, 92–93, 110–13, 115, 136

Apollonius, 31

Ardern, Jacinda, 179, 225

Aristotle, 11, 14, 16, 49, 90–93

Arrian, 12, 28

Assent, 27, 41, 72–76, 78, 222, 237

Attalus the Stoic, 19

Aurelius, Marcus
birth of, 30
challenges of, 33
death of, 34
early life of, 30–31
education of, 30–31
as emperor, 29–39
governance and, 31–32
legacy of, 34, 38–39

philosophy of, 8, 11–14, 28–39, 47–50, 52–54, 57–58, 60–63, 66–69, 76–77, 80–81, 84–88, 95–109, 113–19, 121, 124–27, 130–34, 141–48, 156, 160–78, 180–87, 193, 197–205, 210–13, 219–22, 226–28, 231–33, 236–38, 242, 247, 251–66
plague and, 32, 96, 117, 132, 175
works by, 12, 29–31, 33–39, 49–50, 61, 69, 84, 87, 103, 130, 144, 148, 166, 169–70, 177, 202, 212, 228, 258

Beck, Aaron T., 152

Brady, Tom, 234

Buffett, Warren, 188

Caesar, Augustus, 126

Caesar, Julius, 62, 70, 178

Caligula, Emperor, 19–20

Career, 45, 89, 140–41, 170, 172–75, 188, 231, 246

Cassius, Avidius, 33

Cato the Younger, 14, 62, 70, 88, 178–79, 196, 208, 222–23, 232, 238

Challenges, 7–8, 30–35, 42–48, 56–59, 67–89, 101–5, 117–26, 137–59, 168–99, 209–26, 233–66

Changes, 43–47, 59–60, 80–88, 105, 121–26, 136–37, 153–57, 174–81, 185–89, 200–203, 209–21

Character, 48–71, 93–100, 127–30, 141–49, 184–87, 197–203, 215–18, 228–32, 237, 251, 265

Christianity, 21, 29, 147–52

Chrysippus, 11, 104, 198

Churchill, Winston, 189

Cicero, Marcus Tullius, 14, 191

Claudius, Emperor, 19–20, 248

Cleanthes, 11, 17, 141–42, 198

Cognitive therapies, 80, 152–54

Commodus, Emperor, 34

Community service, 52–54, 60–67, 70–71, 101, 106–9, 127–34, 148, 176–81, 238–39

Comparisons, 203–8, 214

Compassion, 46, 60–63, 83, 101, 129–48, 172–83, 201–10, 224–25, 242, 259, 266

Consistency, 69, 106, 119, 157–58, 197–201, 233, 235–39, 250–53, 258

Contentment, 10–20, 50–55, 64–67, 91–100, 105–15, 157–58, 171, 203–8, 212, 218, 245–49, 265–66. *See also* Happiness

Control, 26–28, 37–38, 40–53, 64–67, 87–88, 112–15, 146–48, 170, 185–87, 218, 260. *See also* Self-control

Cook, Tim, 175

Cosmopolitanism, 127–29, 132, 148, 176, 238

Courage, 16, 48–53, 56–69, 100–104, 139–49, 163, 177, 186, 201, 214, 228–43, 254

Crates of Thebes, 7, 10, 15–16

Criticism, 37, 137–38, 201, 207, 214–15, 217–20, 229

Cynics, 10, 13–17

De Ira (On Anger), 111, 123–24

Death, 7, 26, 36, 46, 79, 82–84, 117–18, 122, 125–26, 160–63, 166, 241–43, 248, 261

Democritus, 91

Detachment, 42–43, 83–86, 131, 165–73, 192–97, 211, 223–24, 233, 238, 246, 253, 257, 260, 265

Determinism, 104–5, 111, 145

Dichotomy of Control, 26–28, 37–38, 40–53, 64–67, 87–88, 112–15, 146–48, 170, 185–87, 218, 260

Diogenes of Sinope, 10

Diognetus, 30

Discipline, 28, 38–41, 58, 64–67, 101, 141–49, 171–79, 188–99, 226, 233–34, 250–53

Discomfort, 16, 51, 56, 67, 121, 141–42, 192–98, 201–3, 246, 256. *See also* Suffering

Discourses of Epictetus, 12, 28

Distractions, 24–25, 64–67, 148, 167, 177, 215–16, 248–49, 252

Domitian, Emperor, 27

Duty, 31–43, 54–61, 68–70, 106–9, 117, 127, 148, 173–76, 190–202, 215, 242, 261

Ego, 37, 82, 219–20

Ellis, Albert, 153

Emotions, managing, 7–8, 37–39, 64–69, 73–93, 96–142, 153–59, 164–77, 182–93, 200–212, 222–29, 237–41, 255–66

Empathy, 60–61, 83, 129–34, 141, 145, 172–75, 182, 210, 225. *See also* Compassion

Enchiridion, 12, 28–29, 86

Endurance, 89, 139–42, 148–51, 163, 187, 191–99, 212, 226–27, 266

Enemies, 209–12

Epictetus
    birth of, 26
    death of, 27
    early life of, 26–27
    education of, 26–27
    later life of, 27
    legacy of, 28–29
    philosophy of, 8, 11–12, 26–31, 40–41, 44–51, 57, 61, 67, 70–79, 86–89, 94–99, 106–10, 113, 116, 121, 125–26, 133, 135, 138, 141–45, 148, 153, 158, 161, 168–69, 174–82, 186, 191, 196–202, 207–11, 214, 221–22, 227–37, 245–56, 259–65
    works by, 12, 28–29, 86

Epicureanism, 10, 13, 92

Epicurus, 10, 92, 179, 198, 203

Escher, M. C., 74

Ethical living, 10–25, 30–38, 50–71, 87–93, 102–5, 127–30, 147–59, 162–63, 167–87, 202, 230–39, 250–57

Eudaimonia, 49, 68–71, 90–93, 98–101, 103, 110–11

Exercise, 141, 195–99, 234, 250–51, 258

External events, 16, 24, 27, 38–59, 77–99, 103–23, 139–48, 153–54, 164–87, 203–10, 215–37, 245–49, 254–60, 265

External goods, 10, 15–16, 49–51, 64–66, 94–97, 120, 223–24, 245–49

Externals, 41–51, 94–97, 139–40, 219–20, 224, 237

Fame, 10, 15–16, 49, 51, 94–97, 154, 203, 230, 233

Fate, 21, 33, 38, 88, 104–7, 116, 143–57, 181, 205–6, 211, 247–48, 265

Ferriss, Tim, 257

Four virtues, 48–71, 101–4, 130–44, 179–81. *See also specific virtues*

Free will, 104–5

Freedom, 8, 10–12, 26–28, 43, 51, 67, 86–93, 110–12, 148, 201, 215–16, 223–24, 254, 265

Friendship, 36, 180, 260–62. *See also* Relationships

Goals, 14, 28, 66, 69, 90–91, 101, 157, 161, 197, 229–34

Gratitude, 36, 161, 166, 203, 244–49, 256, 266

Hadrian, Emperor, 28–31, 126, 228

Happiness, 7–8, 10–24, 48–58, 64–80, 90–115, 123–29, 144–47, 152–87, 201–8, 237–49, 256–66. *See also* Contentment

Health/fitness, 45, 128, 141, 190–99, 234, 250–51, 258

Human contract, 176–79

Human nature, 35, 56, 91, 102–11, 114–18, 155, 225, 266

Humanity, 34, 63, 70, 85, 101, 122, 127–34, 144, 148–51, 155, 176–79

Impermanence, 36, 79, 166, 261. *See also* Death; Mortality

Impressions, 27, 41, 72–76, 78, 98, 191, 222, 237

Indifference, 16, 42–49, 54, 68, 79, 89, 94–95, 110–16, 131–39, 156–58, 173–74, 187–220, 228–37, 246–47

Integrity, 37, 48–51, 62, 69–71, 88, 100, 148–49, 173–84, 201–7, 212–16, 230–39

Interconnectedness, 37, 61–63, 81–83, 102–7, 116, 130, 155, 210

James, LeBron, 258

Jefferson, Thomas, 179

Jesus, 148, 150–51

Jobs, Steve, 163

Judgment, 27, 57–62, 72–89, 99–113, 118–24, 134–38, 153–54, 165, 182–86, 202, 210–25, 235–37

Justice, 16, 32–33, 47–65, 68–70, 93–97, 104–8, 130–39, 148, 167, 177–81, 201–14, 236–39, 252–59

Kennedy, John F., 225

Laërtius, Diogenes, 17

Leadership, 30–38, 157, 172–79, 188–89, 224

Limitations, 45, 156–59, 173, 192, 198, 200, 207

Lives of Eminent Philosophers, 17

Living according to nature, 7, 10, 14–15, 48, 56–58, 90, 103, 106–9, 130, 178

Living in present moment, 24, 100, 120, 124–26, 158–67, 171, 240, 245–53, 261, 266

Logos, 11, 17, 90, 93, 102–5, 107, 111, 130, 145, 148, 150–51, 159, 176

Love, 38, 61, 85, 143–51, 181, 202, 242, 259–62, 265

Lucilius, 12, 20, 22, 53, 100, 120, 162, 206–7, 241–42

Mandela, Nelson, 145

Martyr, Justin, 149

Material possessions, 10, 15–16, 94–97, 120, 245–49. *See also* External goods

Meditation, 83, 120, 250–51, 257–58

Meditations, 12, 29–31, 33, 35–39, 49–50, 61, 69, 84, 87, 103, 130, 144, 148, 166, 169–70, 177, 202, 212, 228, 258

Memento Mori, 82, 160–63, 166

Memorabilia, 15

Merkel, Angela, 179

Mill, John Stuart, 93

Mindfulness, 38, 43, 66, 83, 120–21, 164–67, 170–71, 197, 245–50, 252–58

Minimalism, 190–91, 248–49

Moral character, 48–49, 56–61, 68–71, 115, 127–30, 148–49, 215–18, 237. *See also* Character

Moral consistency, 201, 235–39. *See also* Consistency

Moral integrity, 48, 148–49, 237. *See also* Integrity

Moral Letters to Lucilius, 20, 22, 100, 120, 241–42

Mortality, 7, 26, 36, 46, 79, 160–63, 166, 261. *See also* Death

Nadella, Satya, 175

Natural Questions, 20

Nature, living according to, 7, 10, 14–15, 48, 56–58, 90, 103, 106–9, 130, 178

Navy SEALs, 199

Negative visualization, 120, 124–25, 155, 174, 186, 196, 240–44, 246, 256, 266

Nero, Emperor, 12, 18, 20–21, 26, 95, 176, 211, 248

Nicomachean Ethics, 92

Nietzsche, Friedrich, 116, 143–44

Objectivity, 79, 112–15, 121, 134–37, 165–67, 218, 221–22

Obstacles, 7–8, 101–5, 144–49, 155, 186–87, 226–29, 256, 264–65. *See also* Challenges

Oikeiôsis, 127–32, 134

On Anger, 111, 123–24

On the Happy Life, 20

On the Shortness of Life, 19, 22–23, 125

On Tranquility of Mind, 25

Opinions, 75–80, 87–88, 97, 116, 137–38, 200–218, 221–25, 228

Optimism, 263–66

Panaetius, 11

Passion, 66, 110–11, 115, 133, 136–37, 148, 170, 173–74, 255, 259, 262

Patagonia, Inc., 239

Pathos, 110–11, 137

Paul the Apostle, 150

Peace, 10–14, 37–39, 42–55, 77–115, 122–26, 146, 159, 167–75, 183–89, 206–19, 225–26, 264–65. *See also* Tranquility

Perotti, Niccolò, 29

Personal development, 35–38, 127–30, 168–75, 182–84, 195–99, 204–7, 218–20, 226–36, 250–58, 265

Perspective, 7–8, 51–58, 64–65, 71–89, 112–26, 133–40, 147–65, 180–98, 209–31, 257–65

Plato, 11, 14, 16, 49, 91–92, 156, 181

Posidonius, 11

Premeditatio Malorum, 120, 124–25, 155, 186, 196, 240–44, 266

Present, living in, 24, 100, 120, 124–26, 158–67, 171, 240, 245–53, 261, 266

Priorities, 24–25, 66–67, 115–16, 160, 163, 173, 236

Productivity, 22, 44–47, 79, 122, 137–38, 193–94, 230–32, 257

Psychology, 38, 80, 137, 152–55, 196

Rationality, 7–8, 10–11, 15–17, 36–41, 52–63, 72–73, 90–122, 125–88, 191–227, 237–39, 257–66

Reason, 7–8, 10–11, 15–17, 36–41, 48–59, 66–73, 90–93, 102–11, 127–88, 201–26, 255–66

Reeves, Keanu, 233

Reflections, 25, 33–39, 53, 66–67, 75, 108–9, 120–24, 162–67, 170–71, 201, 236, 254–58

Relationships, 36–38, 45–70, 79, 89, 101, 121–34, 138–51, 170–84, 200–212, 224, 229, 237–42, 259–62

Religion, 21, 29, 147–52, 154

The Republic, 91

Reputation, 28, 40, 65, 97, 120–22, 140, 202, 213–16

Resilience, 7–8, 11–13, 26–29, 38–39, 50–59, 67–71, 86–89, 114–18, 139–78, 184–86, 189–220, 226–34, 253–66

Respect, 61, 71, 130, 172–79, 216, 259–62

Responses, 33–34, 45–59, 72–126, 131–46, 157–75, 180–84, 191, 203, 209–29, 237–47, 255–56

Restraint, 64–67, 111, 192, 196–97, 223

Rufus, Musonius, 27, 107, 148, 167, 192–93, 195–96, 216, 230, 248, 261–62

Rusticus, 31

Sagan, Carl, 85

Saint Ambrose, 149

Self-acceptance, 107–9, 200–207. *See also* Acceptance

Self-awareness, 24, 50–51, 65, 128–29, 167, 170, 201, 254–58

Self-care, 45, 128, 190–99, 234, 250–51, 258

Self-control, 37–41, 47–48, 64–67, 96–99, 108–15, 126, 146–48, 170, 179–87, 192–96, 204–6. *See also* Control

Self-discipline, 28, 38–41, 58, 101, 141, 149. *See also* Discipline

Self-esteem, 200–203

Self-examination, 10, 27, 95, 236–37, 251–55

Self-help, 168–71, 253

Self-improvement, 35–38, 171–75, 182–84, 198–99, 204–7, 218–20, 226–31, 250–58. *See also* Personal development

Self-interest, 128–32

Self-preservation, 128, 131–32

Self-reflection, 38–39, 201, 254–58. *See also* Reflections

Self-sufficiency, 10, 91–92

Self-worth, 201, 219, 227

Seneca
    accomplishments of, 18–21
    birth of, 18
    career of, 18–21
    death of, 21
    early life of, 18–19
    education of, 19
    exile of, 19–20, 117, 248
    later life of, 19–21

legacy of, 21
philosophy of, 8, 11–12, 18–26, 53, 56, 58, 61–70, 76, 81, 85, 90, 93–97, 100, 111–12, 117–20, 123–26, 133–34, 138–39, 141–52, 161–65, 168–76, 180, 183, 186–93, 200–207, 211, 214, 219, 227, 232, 238–55, 260–66
works by, 18–25, 100, 120, 125, 241–42
Sextus, 261
Short, William, 179
Socrates, 9–10, 12–16, 28, 90–93, 156, 176–77, 196, 220, 223, 250, 261
Stockdale, James, 89, 163
Stoicism. *See also specific virtues*
critique of, 156–59
development of, 11–13
explanation of, 7–8
founder of, 7, 9–17, 49, 79, 95, 141–42, 198
misconceptions about, 131, 156–59
modern life and, 8–9, 13, 22–26, 38–39, 51, 62–67, 71, 80, 83–89, 109, 137, 145, 152–59, 163, 171–75, 179, 184–86, 197–99, 207–8, 225, 233–34, 239–40, 248–49, 253–58
origins of, 9–13
principles of, 7–13, 31–39, 168–71
Stress, 42–46, 83–89, 100, 112–19, 123–26, 137, 155, 165–74, 186, 240–44, 257
Suffering, 41, 61, 87–89,

95–99, 110–21, 125–42, 146–55, 185–93, 197–203, 226, 240, 261
Sympatheia, 116
Temperance, 16, 48–52, 58–69, 92–93, 104, 139–40, 177, 201, 214, 236, 254
Tertullian, 149
Theology, 147–51, 159
Thrasea, 248
Time management, 19, 22–25, 125, 162, 251–52
Tranquility, 7, 10–11, 25, 37–39, 50, 77–115, 136, 146, 186–93, 201, 225–26, 244, 261. *See also* Peace
Treatment of others, 7, 47–70, 101, 127–34, 138–48, 174–84, 210–12, 224, 237–42, 259. *See also* Relationships
Tuitert, Mark, 208
Tutu, Desmond, 212
Utilitarianism, 93
Verus, Lucius, 31
"View from above," 81–85, 155. *See also* Perspective
Virtues, 7–24, 32–43, 48–71, 80–111, 130–44, 147–53, 160–87, 190–220, 226–39, 243–66. *See also specific virtues*
Vologases IV, King, 32
Wealth, 10, 14–16, 19–20, 24, 48–54, 94–97, 154, 203, 228–33, 243, 245–49
Will, 27, 40–42, 67, 95, 104–5, 181–82, 192, 197
Winfrey, Oprah, 249
Wisdom, 7–9, 13–17, 22–39, 48–69, 80–104, 119–23, 139–54, 167–84, 201–14, 227–36, 254–66

Workplace, 45, 89, 140–41, 170, 172–75, 188, 231, 246
Worst-case scenarios, 155, 186, 240–44, 266
Xenophon, 15
Yousafzai, Malala, 239
Zeno of Citium
birth of, 14
death of, 17
early life of, 14–15
as founder of Stoicism, 7, 9–11, 14–17, 49, 79, 95, 141–42, 198
influences on, 7, 10–11, 14–16
legacy of, 17
philosophy of, 7, 9–11, 14–17, 49, 79, 95, 141–42, 168, 198